WHAT YOUR COLLEAGUES ARE SAYING . . .

Leader Credibility is a must-read for every educational leader. All too often, school improvement plans and initiatives fail, not on their merits but on the credibility of the leader. Educational leaders need to be strategic about how they contribute to or derail the success of these initiatives, and this book provides a framework for how to build leader credibility and opportunities for structured self-reflection.

Randy Clyde
Middle School Principal
San Bernardino City Unified School District
San Bernardino, CA

This book offers tangible ways to build your leadership credibility and concrete methods for building strong relationships that will cultivate a culture of trust and community.

Betty Zavala
Elementary School Principal, Klein ISD
Spring, TX

I highly recommend this book. Teachers are yearning for great leadership, and this book helps educational leaders analyze the skill set it takes to lead with credibility.

Dawn Massey
Principal, Okaloosa County School District
Fort Walton Beach, FL

The authors share relevant research, illustrations, and tools for self-reflection that can be used to impact the daily work of school leaders. By reading *Leader Credibility*, leaders will be challenged to think more intentionally about how they build trust, competence, dynamism, and immediacy, and how they become more forward thinking.

Alisa Barrett
Director of Instruction, Greenfield Exempted
Village Schools
Greenfield, OH

I cannot overstate the significance of leadership credibility. On a recent livestream, I spent 90 minutes discussing leadership credibility and could have very easily gone for hours more. In their newest collaboration, Douglas Fisher, Nancy Frey, Cathy Lassiter, and Dominique Smith have completed those hours for me. *Leadership Credibility* makes a compelling argument for the significance of school leadership credibility toward overall school leadership effectiveness. Fisher and Frey have written another winner that all school leaders and aspiring school leaders should add to their professional learning.

Baruti Kafele
Retired Principal, Education Consultant, Author

LEADER
credibility

DOUGLAS FISHER
NANCY FREY
CATHY LASSITER
DOMINIQUE SMITH

LEADER
credibility

The Essential Traits of Those Who *Engage, Inspire,* and *Transform*

FOREWORD BY
MICHAEL
FULLAN

CORWIN
Fisher & Frey

FOR INFORMATION:

Corwin

A SAGE Company

2455 Teller Road

Thousand Oaks, California 91320

(800) 233-9936

www.corwin.com

SAGE Publications Ltd.

1 Oliver's Yard

55 City Road

London EC1Y 1SP

United Kingdom

SAGE Publications India Pvt. Ltd.

B 1/I 1 Mohan Cooperative Industrial Area

Mathura Road, New Delhi 110 044

India

SAGE Publications Asia-Pacific Pte. Ltd.

18 Cross Street #10-10/11/12

China Square Central

Singapore 048423

President: Mike Soules

Vice President and
  Editorial Director: Monica Eckman

Senior Acquisitions Editor: Tanya Ghans

Content Development
  Manager: Desirée A. Bartlett

Editorial Assistant: Nyle De Leon

Production Editor: Melanie Birdsall

Typesetter: C&M Digitals (P) Ltd.

Proofreader: Ellen Brink

Cover Designer: Scott Van Atta

Marketing Manager: Morgan Fox

ISBN 978-1-0718-8910-7

Library of Congress Control Number: 2022940985

This book is printed on acid-free paper.

22 23 24 25 26 10 9 8 7 6 5 4 3 2 1

CONTENTS

FOREWORD

by Michael Fullan

Being a devotee of learning from practice, I was pleased to see Douglas Fisher, Nancy Frey, Cathy Lassiter, and Dominique Smith build from establishing what works in fostering learning in the classroom and in school and move toward defining what kind of leadership would best support such learning. When I examine the authors' insights, I can see why certain leadership is geared to success, and I am doubly affirmed when I see the specific leadership traits associated with success. Fisher, Frey, Lassiter, and Smith's findings are totally congruent with our leadership research over the past four decades.

The authors reinforce another feature of our change findings, namely that we need to identify the smallest number of key factors that meet the following criteria: clarity, comprehensiveness, succinctness, and mutual exclusivity (nonoverlapping). The variables, of course, have to end up being crystal clear (understandable) and linked to practice (what effective leaders actually do). Fisher, Frey, Lassiter, and Smith's core components of credibility—trust, competence, dynamism, and immediacy—provide the foundation of effective leadership traits. These traits represent what effective teachers do in relation to their students; leaders, then, have a double responsibility, as they must first be able to recognize the core four components (trust, competence, dynamism, and immediacy) in their teachers, and second, to possess and model such factors in their relationship with teachers.

Another key aspect of leadership we have discovered in our work is the capacity *to be specific* about the practices that make a difference. As with all seemingly clear insights, the leadership meaning is subtle, or, if you like, "nuanced" (Fullan, 2019). The full insight is that effective leaders must help teachers and others achieve *specificity without imposition*. Consider that if you mandate something without buy-in, it will fail. If you get teachers to agree with something in the absence of specific practices, it will also fail. The sophistication lies in the detailed working relationship between school leaders and teachers; it is the clarity and comprehensiveness of this relationship that counts. And therein lies the value of *Leader Credibility: The Essential Traits of Those Who Engage, Inspire, and Transform.*

As I mentioned, the book contains all the key concepts one needs to be a successful leader. The next requirement is that these concepts must be unpacked, both for clarity and for understanding and developing the ideas, and this is the real strength of the book. There are more than 20 instruments—rubrics, diagnostics, survey instruments, and checklists—across the five chapters, all geared to the concepts in the book and keyed to the task of developing leadership credibility and impact. The tools in the introduction, for example, compare factors that compromise leader credibility with those that enhance credibility (Sinha, 2020), provide sample indicators of immediacy with students, and compare instructional and transformational leaders.

It is the four core concepts that constitute the core value of leader credibility: trust, competence, dynamism, and immediacy. They operate as an integrated set. In action, they push the organization forward. They provide guidelines for how leaders should spend their time. As a set, as the authors argue in the last chapter, these concepts constitute "why forward-thinking leadership matters." Here is a book that puts the question of leader credibility in the hands of those who are willing to focus on a small number of interrelated factors, all the while fostering consistent practice in day-to-day implementation.

—Michael Fullan

Professor Emeritus, OISE/University of Toronto

Toronto, Ontario, Canada

ACKNOWLEDGMENTS

Corwin gratefully acknowledges the contributions of the following reviewers:

Alisa Barrett
Director of Instruction
Greenfield Exempted Village Schools
Greenfield, OH

Jakki S. Jethro
Executive Director of Schools
New Hanover County Schools
Wilmington, NC

Dawn Massey
Principal, Okaloosa County School District
Fort Walton Beach, FL

Betty Zavala
Elementary School Principal
Klein ISD
Spring, TX

SETTING
THE STAGE

From Teacher Credibility to Leader Credibility

Marco Caresquero was standing at the front of the room, having just explained that many of the students at their school reported feeling anonymous. According to the data from a recent survey, 48% of the students believed that their teachers did not know their names. Sixty-four percent said that the teachers did not make an effort to get to know them; 56% said that they were treated with respect by the teachers. More than 70% of the students indicated that they did not believe that anyone at school cared if they were absent, yet 82% of them reported feeling proud of their school and 93% said that their parents cared about their education. As Mr. Caresquero reviewed the data, he showed pictures of students, the slides showing face after face of a young person who attended the school.

Mr. Caresquero suggested that they develop a mentoring program, noting, "I know that the overall effect size of mentoring is not very strong. There are some studies, and one meta-analysis with 73 studies, that are more promising, but I understand that this may not impact academic achievement. But stay with me. In the past, we've talked a lot about students' sense of belonging and their well-being, and we know that when students have a strong sense of belonging, the effect size is good. What if we could create a mentoring program that improves belonging rather than focusing the mentoring sessions on tutoring or intervention?"

The principal continued: "Here's my challenge for the entire staff—classified, paraprofessionals, and certificated—as well as for administration. We each accept responsibility for eight students. We meet with them at least weekly, but maybe more often. We talk with them as caring adults. We ask them about their classes and how they are doing, but the focus is on getting to know each student beyond the surface. And when we do, we start to broker relationships with our mentees and other staff at our school."

Projecting the next slide, Mr. Caresquero said, "Here's my challenge. It's an 'ABC.'" The slide listed three goals:

A. **Accept** the challenge of getting to know a small group of students.

B. **Believe** in them. Help them believe they can excel in school.

C. **Commit** to focusing on these students throughout the school year.

"I have lists of students, randomly generated, for anyone who is willing to take on this challenge," Mr. Caresquero added. "I don't have all the logistics figured out, and I'm open to recommendations about the best way that we can make this happen for our students—I just believe that they need us. They need to know that we care and that we see them. If you accept the challenge, please pick up one of the lists at the back of the room as we say goodbye today."

What do you think happened at the end of the meeting? Were the lists of names ignored and left on the back table? Did the staff enthusiastically add this additional job responsibility to their already busy week? Did they pick up a list of names, knowing that they wouldn't really do anything with it but because the principal might be watching? Did they speak out, saying that this was not their responsibility and that they wouldn't do it?

Any of these results could have happened. And this range of responsiveness occurs all the time in reaction to initiative and ideas. The question is, why is it more likely that one school will take such a task on and another won't? Our answer is, in a large part, based on leader credibility: some leaders have developed credibility with teachers and staff members while others have not. Leader credibility influences the climate of the school and the ways in which work is accomplished. In some places, significant amounts of cynicism exist. In other places, fear and mistrust are prevalent. And in other places, there is a spirit of collaboration and a belief that leaders know what they are doing and have the best interests of educators, staff, and students at heart. In other words, the leader is credible and creates a climate in which staff members know that they can learn from this person.

We have to ask: if people choose not to follow you, are you a leader? People choose not to follow when they

- Do not trust the leader

- Question the competence of the leader

- Sense a lack of passion and confidence from the leader

- Do not feel close to, or relatedness with, the leader

- Are not sure where the organization is going and how they fit into the future

PAUSE AND PONDER

▶ Think about two leaders in your professional life, one with strong credibility and one without. Did you choose to follow the one without strong credibility? Were any of the factors on the bulleted list in play for you? What did you notice about the leader who was credible?

COMPONENTS OF CREDIBILITY

The bulleted list above provides a general overview of what we know about credibility. We'll start with a discussion of *teacher credibility*, as there are several studies that outline this idea (e.g., Won & Bong, 2017). The studies can be summed up with one question: do I believe that I can learn from you? The effect size of teacher credibility on student learning is powerful. The average effect size for over 300 influences on learning is 0.40 (www.visiblelearningmetax.com); teacher credibility has an effect size of 1.09. In other words, it is well above average and has the potential to positively impact student learning.

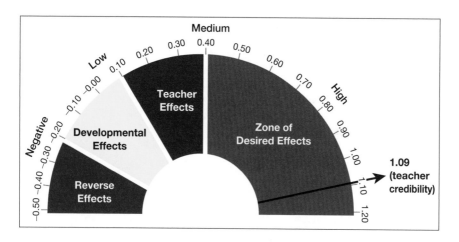

When students believe that they can learn from their teachers, they are much more likely to do so. Interestingly, the same instructional strategy or lesson, delivered in the same way by two different teachers, can have two different impacts if one of the classes of students believes that they can learn from the teacher and the other class does not. In other words, it's not about the specific strategies that are used, even though several strategies have the potential to impact learning—it's students believing that they can learn from their teachers. When they do, the tools that are used by the teacher are more likely to have an impact. Thus, some minimally effective approaches might ensure learning more than strategies with a greater likelihood of impact but delivered by teachers whose students do not think that they can learn from those teachers. In part, this is why we, and Visible Learning® in general, focus so much attention on determining impact and talking more about learning than about teaching.

As leaders, part of our role is to monitor teacher credibility and help those who struggle in this area to develop and grow. Far too often, however, leaders focus on instructional strategies and attempt to coach a teacher on getting better at using specific strategies. There is nothing wrong with building teachers' toolboxes and ensuring that the approaches they use have a strong likelihood of impact. But failing to attend to teacher credibility and the signs that the students do not believe that they can learn from a given teacher will result in students' lack of progress in their learning. Without attention to teacher credibility, learning is left to chance even in the presence of quality instruction. In our previous work (e.g., Fisher et al., 2020), we organized the teacher credibility construct into four areas: trust, competence, dynamism, and immediacy. We'll review each of those before moving into a discussion about leader credibility.

Trust

Honest and *reliable* come to mind when we talk about teachers establishing trust with students. As we will explore further in Chapter 1, there is more to trust in schools, but for now, we'll note the importance of students knowing that their teachers are honest and reliable. When trust is present, students are more likely to take risks in their learning and feel comfortable making mistakes. When trust is broken, students are wary of their teachers and they play it safe. Leaders notice the trusting, honest, and growth-producing relationships between teachers and students and coach them when trust needs to be established, maintained, or repaired.

Consider Susan Carter, a math teacher whose students were not performing well despite the fact that the lessons were generally good and the strategies used were appropriate. Her students rarely volunteered to answer questions in class, and they refrained from sitting in the front seats. When asked, students said that they didn't really know her or trust her.

The principal suggested that she stand at the door and greet students by name as they entered the classroom. Ms. Carter's first reaction was to protest, "But I need to get my materials ready and take attendance." The principal suggested she try it for three weeks and see if it made a difference. It didn't even take that long. Within a week, several students were shaking her hand or giving her a high five or a fist bump when entering the room. By the end of the three weeks, the environment in Ms. Carter's class had changed. Students were volunteering, taking risks, and joking with her. About six weeks later, when a student acted out in class, several peers said, "Hey, we don't do that here. She's cool. Let her teach." When Ms. Carter shared this story with her principal, she noted, "I didn't really think about the power of students trusting me. I have a whole different relationship with my students now. I was thinking about quitting because I wasn't seeing results. It's so different now. Thank you."

PAUSE AND PONDER

▶ How can you identify teachers who need to focus on trust? How might you help them increase trust in their classroom?

Competence

Trusting relationships are important, but they are not enough to ensure that students learn at deep levels. Knowing that teachers care is important, but we all know caring educators who cannot teach. They mean well and do the best that they know how to do at the time, but their instructional repertoires are not strong enough to ensure that all students learn. And students know this. They spend hundreds of hours with their teachers and are acutely aware of those who engage them in meaningful learning tasks and those who cannot. Recall the situation with Ms. Carter and her work on trust: her classroom instruction was strong, but her students did not know her or trust her.

When it comes to instruction, some basic moves make a difference. We have argued that the gradual release of responsibility is a way to categorize teacher moves that increase the likelihood of students learning (Fisher & Frey, 2021). Teacher clarity requires that students know the following:

- What am I learning today?
- Why am I learning this?
- How will I know that I learned it?

And the tasks that we ask students to complete should align with those responses. We see categories of teacher moves that can be presented in any order that allow students to learn (see Figure I.1). In reality, these moves are cyclical and recursive. A teacher may model for students at several points in the lesson, and students may engage in collaborative tasks many times. Note that there is a wide range of instructional strategies that can be used, and we should not hold any strategy in higher esteem than students' learning. We focus not on the specific strategies that a teacher is using, but rather guide their selection of tools while monitoring impact.

FIGURE I.1 ACCESS POINTS FOR THE GRADUAL RELEASE OF RESPONSIBILITY

ACCESS POINT	DEFINITION	EXAMPLE STRATEGIES
The first access point is teacher modeling of critical thinking.	This phase provides students access to the thinking of an "expert" that they will try on throughout the lesson.	• Shared reading • Read-aloud • Think-aloud • Direct instruction • Worked examples • Write-aloud • Interactive writing • Demonstration • Lecture

(Continued)

(Continued)

ACCESS POINT	DEFINITION	EXAMPLE STRATEGIES
The second access point is achieved through guided instruction.	Using robust questions, prompts, and cues, teachers scaffold students' understanding and provide students with the teacher-supported experiences they need to learn.	• Scaffolded reading • Close reading • Cognitively guided instruction • Whole-class guided practice
The third access point is collaborative learning.	These tasks encourage students to interact with one another in order to develop a deeper understanding of what they are learning. Sometimes there is individual accountability within the task (such as jigsaw), and other times there is not (such as in think-pair-share).	• Literature circles or book clubs • Reciprocal teaching • ReQuest • Table topics • Listening stations • Jigsaw • Five-word summaries • Peer-assisted reflection
The fourth access point is independent learning.	Students practice and apply what they have learned on their own, either in class or after class.	• Independent reading • Daily writing (journals, essays, short stories, poetry, etc.) • Homework • Interactive videos • Notetaking

SOURCE: Adapted from Fisher, Frey, Amador, and Assof (2019).

Our point here is that teachers need to be seen as competent by their students, and the instructional tools teachers use help establish that competence. Of course, teachers also need to know their subject matter and recognize that errors are part of the learning process. And when teachers change their instructional strategies too frequently, students start to wonder if their teachers know how to teach. Competence is an area that most leaders focus on. We want to help teachers reach their potential through using evidence-based practices and monitoring impact. Having said that, an expert teacher who does not earn the trust of students, who does not have passion, and who is not relatable probably will not get very good outcomes.

PAUSE AND PONDER

▶ How can you identify teachers who need to focus on competence? How might you help them increase their skills?

Dynamism

Active, fast-paced learning environments in which students are challenged and supported characterize this third aspect of teacher credibility. We are not saying that you have to dress in a toga during the Greek-Roman unit or stand on a desk and bounce around excitedly (unless that is your personality)—we are saying that the learning environment should be dynamic and students should get caught up in the excitement of learning. In part, this is where teachers' passion comes through. When a teacher is passionate about what they are teaching *and* passionate about students' learning, the environment is likely to be dynamic.

There are many things that kill the vibe of a classroom, such as public humiliation of a student, terrible visuals and presentations, monotone presentations, boring tasks, and the like. Students appreciate a cognitive challenge and knowing that their teacher can support their learning. Students also appreciate learning experiences that the teacher is excited about and that are relevant to students. We are not suggesting that teachers simply say, "You'll need this in the real world"— isn't going to school the "real world"? And being told that you might be able to use this someday in the future is probably not that motivating. Instead, students want to know the answer to the second clarity question that we posed in the previous section: why am I learning this? Teachers who exhibit dynamism have no problem with students answering this question and seeing their learning as relevant.

Alec Jesperson's students, for instance, tended to do really well in English language arts but not so well in mathematics. In fact, his students performed significantly lower in mathematics compared with students in other classes at his school and well below the district average. Mr. Jesperson followed the pacing guide and curriculum that the school and district adopted, and when he was observed teaching, it was obvious that his students trusted him and that the strategies he used were similar to those in other classes. But there was a difference in the classes themselves. During English language arts, Mr. Jesperson was very animated and asked students follow-up questions. The texts he selected were interesting and relevant to the questions that the class had voted on, such as "Is fair always equal?" The class focused on new words and each student had a vocabulary self-collection journal; they talked about words and how to pronounce them and what they mean. When students were writing, soft music played in the background and Mr. Jesperson met with individual students and small groups. He was clearly passionate about their writing and remembered things that students had written in the past, even bringing them up during conferences.

Mathematics instruction, however, was very different. It was almost as if Mr. Jesperson was a different person. He seemed almost robotic. He explained the content using worked examples and guided instruction, just like his colleagues. He had students talk about their work and then had students complete their individual assignments. He walked around the room as students worked, correcting their mistakes and prompting students' thinking. But it was as if the joy of the English language arts classroom was gone and Mr. Jesperson was trying to get through the rest of the day.

The students noticed this as well. They said things like "Math is boring" and "Why do we have to learn this?" The lack of dynamism and passion during mathematics was noticeable and likely contributed to the lack of achievement in this area. This teacher with high credibility in English language arts had little credibility in mathematics. The principal asked if Mr. Jesperson thought that math should be moved to the morning, when he was fresher. Mr. Jesperson responded, "I don't think that's it. I just don't feel confident in mathematics. I don't have the same passion as I do for my students' literacy. I found math hard in school, and I can't remember ever having fun during math."

The principal, who was fairly new to the school, suggested that Mr. Jesperson attend an upcoming mathematics conference and that he partner with the special education teacher during his mathematics class. "I'm thinking that having Yasmine Lopez in your class every day during mathematics might help. You two could plan and talk about making the content more interesting, and maybe her passion for numeracy will help you," the principal said. "You have the content and strategies down. I think you are ready for a breakthrough in your students' mathematical understandings. And, if it doesn't work in a few weeks, we can try some other things. I'm totally open. I just want to help you see the potential."

The conference was an amazing experience for Mr. Jesperson. He met passionate mathematics educators who had so many ideas for inviting students into the world of mathematics. At the end of one session, Mr. Jesperson approached the presenter and said, "I wish you had been my teacher. I loved your examples and how you had us working. I learned a lot. Could we stay in touch?" The presenter agreed and Mr. Jesperson was very pleased to tell his principal about this.

Mr. Jesperson also partnered with Ms. Lopez, and they talked through the lessons. Mr. Jesperson saw the passion that Ms. Lopez had and stepped up his game, telling her, "I want our students to have a better experience. It's on me. I need to bring the passion I see in you to the students." And he did. The impact was almost immediate. A student said, "That was the coolest. We had to figure out when it was best to rent a boat. We learned about the price and how it changes because when it's too cold, why would you want a boat? It was really hard, but our group did the best."

PAUSE AND PONDER

► How can you identify teachers who need to focus on dynamism? How might you help them find their passion and create an engaging learning environment?

Immediacy

The final area of teacher credibility is immediacy, which is a term used to convey a sense of relatedness. Simply said, some teachers are more approachable than others. Some teachers clearly demonstrate to students a sense of connection. This is both physical and psychological. Some teachers never get physically close, within arm's reach, of some students. Some teachers only high-five or handshake some students and not others. Some teachers are emotionally distant and not relatable at all. And some teachers have differential treatment of students who are not achieving well.

In fact, there are specific behaviors that teachers display when they believe that students are low achieving (Good, 1987). Students who are perceived to be low achieving

- Are criticized more often for failure

- Are praised less frequently

- Receive less feedback

- Are called on less often

- Have less eye contact from the teacher

- Have fewer friendly interactions with the teacher

- Experience acceptance of their ideas less often

There is another term for this: a "chilly" classroom climate in which some students do not feel they are valued and instead feel that "their presence . . . is at best peripheral, and at worst an unwelcome intrusion" (Hall & Sandler, 1982, p. 3). Imagine that you're not currently achieving very well, for whatever reason. And then your teacher interacts with you in the ways described in the list above. How could you possibly achieve? When immediacy is not present in the class, otherwise amazing instructional strategies are not likely to impact learning.

Leaders are responsible for noticing the immediacy in the classroom. We have a brief checklist for some behaviors to notice that can suggest that teacher credibility is compromised in terms of immediacy (see Figure I.2). We suggest identifying three students who are not currently achieving well and observing the classroom from their perspective. If immediacy has been compromised, it's time to take action so that all students have an equitable chance at learning. Interestingly and importantly, the actions that constitute immediacy are generally subconscious and unconscious; it's not that the vast majority of teachers intend to do this. And when the issues are brought to their attention, teachers change. When they do, their credibility increases and student learning is more likely to improve.

FIGURE I.2 SAMPLE INDICATORS OF IMMEDIACY

INTERACTION	STUDENT 1	STUDENT 2	STUDENT 3
Was the student greeted by name when they entered the classroom?			
How many times did the teacher use their name (not as a correction) during the session?			
Did the teacher ask them a critical thinking question related to the content?			
Did the teacher ask them a personal question?			

(Continued)

(Continued)

INTERACTION	STUDENT 1	STUDENT 2	STUDENT 3
Did the teacher pay them a compliment?			
How many times did the teacher provide them with praise for learning performance?			
Did the teacher get physically close (within arm's reach) to them?			

SOURCE: Adapted from Fisher et al. (2021).

PAUSE AND PONDER

► How can you identify teachers who need to focus on immediacy? How might you help them develop connections with students?

NOT JUST TEACHERS

We have focused considerable space on teacher credibility in this introduction because it can change and positively impact student learning. And teachers who have strong credibility with their students like their jobs better and are much more likely to remain in the profession. We believe that the same is true for leaders. We cannot point to any educational research on leader credibility, but the business literature is filled with studies and recommendations about leader credibility (e.g., Hill, 2018).

For example, Williams et al. (2018) note that leader credibility is the antecedent of transformational leadership. In education, instructional leadership is more powerful than transformational leadership when it comes to student learning. The effect sizes are worth noting. The overall effect of transformational leaders is 0.11, whereas the overall effect of instructional leaders is 0.42. As Hattie (2015) notes, referencing the work of Robinson et al. (2008):

> *Transformational leaders* focus more on teachers. They set a vision, create common goals for the school, inspire and set direction, buffer staff from external demands, ensure fair and equitable staffing, and give teachers a high degree of autonomy.
>
> In contrast, *instructional leaders* focus more on students. They're concerned with the teachers' and the school's impact on student learning and instructional issues, conducting classroom observations, ensuring professional development that enhances student learning, communicating high academic standards, and ensuring that all school environments are conducive to learning. (p. 37)

Others have argued that an integrated approach to transformational and instructional leadership is necessary. For example, Marks and Printy (2003) note that "when transformational and shared instructional leadership coexist in an integrated form of leadership, the influence on school performance, measured by the quality of its pedagogy and the achievement of its students, is substantial" (p. 370). Figure I.3 provides an overview of instructional and transformational leadership and how they are complementary to each other.

FIGURE I.3   COMPARING INSTRUCTIONAL AND TRANSFORMATIONAL LEADERSHIP

INSTRUCTIONAL LEADERSHIP	BOTH	TRANSFORMATIONAL LEADERSHIP
EXPECTATIONS		
• Focuses on articulating and communicating clear school goals • Positions principal to seek to limit uncertainty	• Create a school culture focused on the improvement of teaching and learning • Are goal oriented	• Promotes clear vision, creating shared school goals • Seeks to envision and create the future by synthesizing and extending the aspirations of the members of the organization • Requires a higher tolerance for ambiguity and uncertainty from the principal
FOCUS		
• Focuses on coordinating curriculum, supervising and evaluating instruction, monitoring student progress, and protecting instructional time • Focuses on curriculum and instruction	• Focus on organizing and providing a wide range of activities aimed at the development of the staff • Include high expectations	• Focuses on developing the organization's capacity to innovate • Focuses on intellectual stimulation • Positions principal to create conditions conducive to everyone taking a leadership role • Influences people by building from the bottom up rather than from the top down
LEADERSHIP STYLE		
• Transactional • Features strong, directive leadership • Focuses on first-order change	• Feature skillful leadership • Focus on being a visible presence in the school	• Transformational • Features distributed leadership

INSTRUCTIONAL LEADERSHIP	BOTH	TRANSFORMATIONAL LEADERSHIP
LEADERSHIP STYLE		
• Positions principal as the center of expertise and authority • Focuses on improvement of student academic outcomes • Features hands-on principals, hip-deep in curriculum and instruction		• Generates second-order effects, increases the capacity of others to produce first-order effects on learning • Produces changes in people rather than promoting specific instructional strategies

SOURCE: Slade and Gallagher (2021).

PAUSE AND PONDER

▶ After reviewing the information in Figure I.3, what are your strengths? Are you balancing transformational and instructional leadership?

Our point here is to suggest that leader credibility is an important construct that has been missing from conversations in education. Drawing from the business and other professional literature, Sinha (2020) suggests that leaders ask themselves questions and reflect on their responses. Modified for education, these questions might include the following:

- Do the people in your school or district view you as being believable?

- Do the people in your school or district have confidence that you will do the right thing?

- Do the people in your school or district believe that you have the overall organization's interests and employees' interests in mind while making strategic decisions?

- Do people view you as being trustworthy?

Sinha also notes actions that detract from leader credibility as well as actions that enhance credibility (see Figure I.4).

FIGURE I.4 ENHANCING AND COMPROMISING
LEADER CREDIBILITY

FACTORS THAT ENHANCE LEADER CREDIBILITY	FACTORS THAT COMPROMISE LEADER CREDIBILITY
• Focusing on long-term success • Developing foresight • Streamlining operations • Being consistent • Modeling the way	• Inaction • Indecisiveness • Inconsistency • Incoherent communication • Self-serving actions • Treating people poorly

SOURCE: Sinha (2020).

And Sinha sums it up by suggesting that leaders should "keep your promises, do what you say you will, give credit where it is due, acknowledge mistakes, don't talk about others behind their back, don't withhold information, don't belittle others, be consistent and be accountable" (Sinha, 2020).

Note that the factors we discussed regarding teacher credibility come into play for leaders. Trust, competence, dynamism, and immediacy contribute to the credibility you have as a leader. When you have credibility, employee confidence is high, people work hard because they believe in the organization and its mission, and they demonstrate acceptance of the leader. In fact, school improvement hinges on the leader's credibility because the leader cannot teach all the children in the school. The leader's role is about creating the conditions that foster each educator's ability to be their best. As Manna (2015) reminds us, leaders can be magnifiers and multipliers of effective instruction. When we are credible, we can realize that potential.

But it's more than effective instruction and student learning. Educator and student well-being are also important. Again, leader credibility comes into play in this area as well. Credible leaders create conditions that are safe for people to be vulnerable—safe for people to take risks and have pride in what they do, and safe when mistakes are made. In fact, as business professor Anderson (cited in Alt, 2019) notes, "It all hinges on the leader's credibility."

Anderson's research, again, not specific to education, suggests that competent leaders

- Emphasize the future

- Prioritize employees

- Take action and initiative

- Communicate effectively

- Gain knowledge and experience

And Anderson notes that trustworthy leaders

- Communicate and act in a consistent manner

- Protect the organization and employees

- Embody the organization's vision and values

- Consult with and listen to key educational partners

- Communicate openly with others

- Value employees

Thus, when we apply the credibility lens to leaders, we need to add a forward focus. Yes, leaders need to be trustworthy, competent, and dynamic and display immediacy. In addition, leaders must have a vision for the future, keep the team moving forward, and help each employee see their role in creating that future.

CONCLUSION

Leader credibility is an important topic that has been investigated widely in a number of professions. In education, we know that credible leaders are important, but there isn't evidence about the power of this impact. To our thinking, credibility is required if leaders are going to support teachers and students to reach their fullest potential.

When you hear a term like *school leader*, it's understandable to immediately think about principals and administrators with formal titles. But leaders take quite a few forms. In addition to site leaders, there are those who lead district departments and units, from curriculum to student services. And there are lots of teacher-leaders who serve as grade-level or department chairs, as well as instructional coaches with leadership responsibilities. If any of these describe your role, this book is for you.

In the chapters that follow, we will invite you to reflect on your current self in terms of each aspect of leader credibility.

- Chapter 1 focuses on **trust**

- Chapter 2 focuses on **competence**

- Chapter 3 focuses on **dynamism**

- Chapter 4 focuses on **immediacy**

- Chapter 5 focuses on **forward thinking**

We recognize that it takes time to build or rebuild credibility. People form their opinions of you and your credibility through their direct interactions with you, as well as from their indirect observations of your actions and reactions. Join us in exploring this critical aspect of leadership—one that opens doors for leaders to accomplish their goals and create the schools our staff and students deserve.

CHAPTER 1

....

TRUSTWORTHINESS IN LEADERSHIP

Are you trustworthy in the eyes of others? The ability to trust in a leader—whether a leader of teams, schools, or units—is crucial for an organization to work. Distrust is like sand in the gears, as it becomes the unplanned effort that saps the collective strength of the team. Our human need to determine whether we trust is fundamental to our survival. Early humans had to decide whose model to follow in order to find shelter, avoid poisonous plants, and elude predators. Staff have to decide whose model to follow in order to invest in a healthy school climate, avoid legal missteps, and build learners who can reach their aspirations. Leaders convey their trustworthiness through actions that authentically convey caring for others in the school environment, by being consistent and ethical in interactions, and by demonstrating a level of competence in the matters at hand.

Before going further, we invite you to self-assess your credibility as a leader. It can be tempting to run through these items quickly, marking off *Always* for each statement. We encourage you to reflect on actions you have taken *in the last 30 days* to invest in your trustworthiness as a leader (see Figure 1.1).

FIGURE 1.1 TRUSTWORTHINESS SELF-ASSESSMENT

ITEM #	SURVEY ITEM	3 ALWAYS	2 SOMETIMES	1 RARELY	0 NEVER
	TRUSTWORTHINESS				
1.	I make intentional efforts to empathize with teachers and staff by asking how they are feeling and showing care and concern for them as individuals.				
2.	I ensure staff and other key team members know that I became a school leader to learn with and from them and that I enjoy my job most when they achieve.				
3.	I believe in the abilities and motivations of the staff and students.				
4.	I follow through on promises and statements I make to teachers, students, and parents.				
5.	I ensure that I provide accurate, credible information to all educational partners in the school community.				

TRUSTWORTHINESS					
ITEM #	SURVEY ITEM	3 ALWAYS	2 SOMETIMES	1 RARELY	0 NEVER
6.	I create a risk-free climate where teachers and students can learn from mistakes and respect each other in learning.				
Mean for Trustworthiness *(Total divided by 6)*					

In this chapter, as well as those that follow, we'll start off with a self-assessment, followed by a REAL (Realistic, Effortful, Authentic, and Learning-focused) Reflection. Notice that we didn't say "learn*er*-focused." These thought exercises are for you to support your own learning.

REAL REFLECTION

Which of the indicators of trustworthiness are strengths for you?

Which of the indicators present growth opportunities?

What conclusions are you drawing about your trustworthiness?

Whom can you enlist to support you in strengthening your trustworthiness and thus building your credibility?

THE RESEARCH ON TRUSTWORTHINESS

Trust is the currency of leadership. Without trusting relationships within the organization, forward motion grinds to a halt. The groundbreaking work conducted by the Consortium on Chicago School Research demonstrated nearly two decades ago that social trust is necessary for any school improvement effort to thrive. Researchers spent four years with 400 elementary schools observing the ways principals, teachers, students, and community members resolved problems and implemented reforms. To do so, the researchers conducted interviews, observed classrooms, and analyzed meeting notes. They compared their analyses of relational trust (trust between individuals and groups of individuals) to the reading and mathematics test scores over a five-year period. It should come as no surprise that those school communities with high degrees of relational trust made significant progress. Comparatively, "a school with a low score on relational trust at the end of our study had only a one-in-seven chance of demonstrating improved academic productivity" (Bryk & Schneider, 2004, p. 43). In the educational space, note Bryk and Schneider, relational trust occurs as a result of the following:

- **Mutual respect** between parties, especially when there is disagreement or conflict

- **Personal regard,** demonstrated through warmth and caring about others; openness, sharing personal stories, and gentle humor are ways in which we show our personal regard for others

- **Competence in core responsibilities,** as each member of the school community has specific role responsibilities, and all are in turn dependent on one another's competent execution of those duties (what does it mean to be a great teacher/student/leader/family at our school?)

- **Personal integrity,** the final component of relational trust and a function of a person's honesty and reliability; the fundamental measure of how we determine whether a person deserves our trust (in an educational setting, this is perceiving that colleagues have the welfare of students in mind)

Their description of relational trust as "the connective tissue that holds improving schools together" is evidenced in more recent research on trust's role in school innovation (Bryk & Schneider, 2002, p. 144). A 2020 study of 79 schools found that there were three preconditions for innovation: collective teacher efficacy, academic press (a school's emphasis on learning and academic excellence), and relational trust. Further, relational trust had a direct impact on whether collective teacher efficacy and academic press existed (Schwabsky et al., 2020). In other words, a school organization's openness to new ideas and experimentation is predicated on whether there is a network of trust among faculty, students, leaders, and families.

It is difficult to imagine how a school can improve without a willingness to innovate. Trust, it seems, is the keystone of the arch of reform. Yet most school innovation efforts fail to acknowledge the instrumental role that relational trust plays in any initiative. Instead, there is an outsized emphasis on the content and the logistics of the effort and how it will be monitored and so on. These are vital concerns, to be sure. But the elephant in the room—whether there is a sufficient level of trust to sustain the effort—is rarely examined. If the innovation fails, the fault is attributed to the content, and then a new initiative begins. But consider those findings from Chicago: organizations with low levels of relational trust had a 14% chance of achieving success in their reading and math initiatives. There is little doubt that educators worked hard on those failed efforts. But without a sufficient level of resource—trust—the likelihood that their work would deliver desired results was significantly diminished. Connective tissue, indeed.

TRUSTWORTHINESS AND CREDIBILITY

Much has been written about what constitutes a trustworthy individual. For us, Tschannen-Moran's (2004) five facets of trustworthiness in educators—benevolence, honesty, reliability, openness, and competence—work well as an explanation of how we convey to others that we are deserving of their trust. Whether leading a team as a department or grade-level chair, acting as an instructional coach, or holding more formal leadership positions at the site and district levels, educators will find that these five facets act upon and enhance one another.

Let's take the first one, which is benevolence. Being on guard is a protective factor that is baked into our very nature as humans.

We need to be reasonably sure that another has our best interests in mind. In leadership, benevolence is expressed through actions that demonstrate care and concern for others over the long term. There is an ethical component to benevolence, expressed in the form of honesty. This is perhaps the dimension most people think of when they consider trust. It is natural to distrust someone who is deceitful and seeks to obscure the truth from others. We measure a person's track record of honesty to make judgments about their character and integrity.

The third facet of trustworthiness is reliability, which is related to honesty. A reliable person is true to their word and follows through. If they can't deliver on a promise, they own it and take responsibility. In addition, they are consistent and steady in their actions and reactions. Openness is the fourth dimension. This is the extent to which information is shared and disclosed, with discretion applied in what is shared. A person who overshares or violates the confidentiality of another person (even when it's not you) is not viewed as trustworthy. One is likely to think, "If they told me that information about Brad, what are they saying about me?" On the other hand, appropriate levels of disclosure and information sharing signal reciprocal trust between individuals.

The final factor, and one we will explore more thoroughly in the next chapter, is competence. No matter how benevolent, honest, reliable, and open a person is, if we do not perceive them as being competent at the task at hand, we are unlikely to trust them to get the job done. We rely on the expertise of others to make decisions about our personal and professional lives. When faced with a dilemma, we turn to those we see as being competent to seek advice and guidance.

PAUSE AND PONDER

► Relational trust begins with you as a leader. Why is trust in the leader so crucial? What current strengths regarding relational trust exist at your site?

WHAT HUMANS NEED: AUTONOMY

School organizations are composed of people experiencing a wide range of stages in their identity. Take a typical elementary school as an example: there are likely to be four-year-olds in the transitional kindergarten classroom, 17-year-olds on campus doing work related to their career and technical education (CTE) course in their education pathway, a few young adults from the university completing their practicum, and members of the staff in their late twenties and in the early stages of their career working alongside middle- and late-career colleagues. Yet all of them have an important challenge in common: they seek autonomy.

Autonomy is the ability to make choices and decisions, which contributes to motivation and goal-directed behavior. It is an integral part of self-determination theory, which relies on three dimensions: autonomy, competence, and relatedness (Ryan & Deci, 2000). Ryan and Deci note that "human beings can be proactive and engaged or, alternatively, passive and alienated, largely as a function of the social conditions in which they develop and function" (2000, p. 68). In other words, when these conditions are present, motivation increases. Consider what we know about what works for ourselves, our students, and our organization:

- **Autonomy** to make choices and decisions, which contributes to a sense of agency to achieve goals

- **Competence** to demonstrate skills and develop new ones

- **Relatedness** to others through social bonding such that one doesn't feel alone

Trustworthy leaders create a climate such that the people in them can achieve a sufficient level of autonomy in their lives. We'll focus specifically on teacher autonomy as a function of leadership by first discussing what it *isn't*. Teacher autonomy is not a free-for-all in an environment that says it's fine to close your classroom door and do whatever. We have legal and professional obligations regarding curriculum, expectations for how children are treated, and requirements about the structure of the school day and school year. It matters that we all agree that school starts at 7:30 a.m., that we have supervision responsibilities to keep students safe, and that we adhere to contractual and licensure regulations.

Teacher autonomy touches on four crucial elements that, in turn, contribute to a trusting school climate. Drawing from a review of the literature on teacher autonomy, Gwaltney (2012) highlighted these factors (quoted in Grant et al., 2020):

- Classroom control over student teaching and assessment

- Schoolwide influence over organizational and staff development

- Classroom control over curriculum development

- Schoolwide influence over school mode of operation

But there are two types of errors leaders can make that undermine one's perceived trustworthiness as it relates to a climate of teacher autonomy. One is that we can veer too far in the direction of control. There are practices that crush teacher autonomy, and many of them are a direct result of leadership that is not trustworthy. Ruling by decree rather than seeking consensus is a sure recipe for disaster. It is demoralizing for educators when they feel they have no voice in decisions that directly impact their teaching. Teacher turnover and attrition are linked to teacher autonomy. Those feeling a loss of autonomy may move to another school where they have more (Torres, 2014) or leave the profession altogether (Glazer, 2018).

A climate of supportive teacher autonomy is also not one that veers in the opposite direction. A laissez-faire approach where team and site leaders are rarely involved in classroom operations is not going to do anyone much good, either. One of the interesting things about teacher autonomy is that it is developmental in nature, just like autonomy with young people. The amount of autonomy granted to the four-year-olds in the building is going to be different from that of the 17-year-olds working on their CTE pathway requirements, even though they are in the same building. It turns out that the adults in the building require different levels of autonomy depending on their proficiency.

A graduated teacher autonomy framework provides guidance for team leaders, instructional coaches, and site leaders in considering the varied needs of the staff they support and supervise (Grant et al., 2020). Rather than a one-size-fits-all approach, which is likely to alienate highly proficient educators while leaving novices with less support than they need, this framework considers proficiency across four dimensions: planning and preparation, classroom environment, instruction, and professional responsibilities. Importantly, proficiency should not be conflated with experience, with broad assumptions that a teacher with 20 years of experience automatically is more capable than one with 10 years of experience. This framework draws from the language of the Danielson teacher evaluation system, a widely used measure in many districts (see Figure 1.2).

FIGURE 1.2 ANCHORS OF THE GRADUATED TEACHER AUTONOMY FRAMEWORK

EXAMPLE COMPONENTS (DANIELSON, 2007)	BEGINNING PROFICIENCY → LESS AUTONOMY	MASTERED PROFICIENCY → MORE AUTONOMY
PLANNING AND PREPARATION		
• Knowledge of content and pedagogy • Setting instructional outcomes • Designing instruction and assessment	• Lesson plan templates provided by administration and/or specialists • Lesson plan submissions and weekly planning sessions for feedback and review with administrators and/or specialists	• Choice of lesson plan template • No submission or meeting requirements

(Continued)

(Continued)

EXAMPLE COMPONENTS (DANIELSON, 2007)	BEGINNING PROFICIENCY → LESS AUTONOMY	MASTERED PROFICIENCY → MORE AUTONOMY
CLASSROOM ENVIRONMENT		
• Establishing a culture of learning • Managing student behavior • Managing classroom procedures	• Prescribed behavior management system (e.g., PBIS) • Mandated standard procedures and norms • Blackboard configuration	• Choice of behavior management system • Choice of procedures and norms • Choice of blackboard configuration
INSTRUCTION		
• Engaging students in learning • Using questioning and discussion techniques	• Prescribed scripted curriculum • Mandated professional development • Administrator walkthroughs and feedback sessions	• Choice of methodology and approach based on content standards • Administrator walkthroughs optional
PROFESSIONAL RESPONSIBILITIES		
• Participating in professional development • Participating in professional communities • Communicating with families and the school community	• Prescribed professional community involvement (e.g., PLCs) • Prescribed professional development modules • Family communication logs, oversight by a peer mentor	• Opportunity for leadership roles within professional communities (PLCs, grade-level chairs, school and district committees, etc.) • Opportunity for peer mentoring roles for other teachers

NOTE: PBIS = positive behavior incentive system; PLC = professional learning committee or community. Scales are according to each of the four domains of teaching: planning and preparation, classroom environment, instruction, and professional responsibilities (Danielson, 2007).

SOURCE: Grant et al. (2020, p. 104). Used with permission.

Lisa Willis was the science department chair of her large high school and was released part time to serve as an instructional coach. During the school year, Ms. Willis adopted a graduated autonomy framework as a lens for her support of teachers. "My colleagues have quite a range of expertise in what they bring to the classroom," she explained. "One of my colleagues is a National Board Certified teacher and has so much knowledge about curriculum planning. I encouraged her to serve on the new science adoption committee for the district. Having said that, she feels that she needs more support on our school's restorative practices initiative, so that's where I'm focusing my support."

Ms. Willis contrasted this kind of support with another colleague who was new to the school district but not to the profession. "I've been meeting with him to establish a trusting relationship. I guess he felt kind of burned from his last job," she said. "I got him to open up about his challenges by sharing some of my own professional struggles. He's more recently been seeking support about instruction, which is great. We do quite a bit at this school with teacher clarity, which is a new practice for him." Ms. Willis's use of a more tailored approach to providing differentiated coaching supports to colleagues is building her trustworthiness. "I'm noticing that people are feeling 'seen' in terms of who they are and what they need. I read a blog recently that said that things humans need at work: 'I matter. I belong. I'm enabled. I contribute. I'm respected' [Wai, n.d.]. I'm keeping those in mind as I interact as a coach."

PAUSE AND PONDER

▶ How might a graduated autonomy framework enhance trustworthiness at your site? Whom might you enlist?

LEADERSHIP PRACTICES THAT CONVEY AND DERAIL TRUST

Ms. Willis's reminder about the common needs of people in the workplace transcends the role and responsibilities of the adults in the building. We remember an interaction at a middle school between Ryan Watkins, the dean of students, and the lunch monitors. There had been a series of incidents in the lunchroom, and Mr. Watkins was charged with responding. The lunch monitors were frustrated, too, but Mr. Watkins failed to acknowledge that. Instead, he launched into a diatribe: "I don't know what's been going on down here, but the kids are out of control and you're not managing them the way you should." You can imagine the lunch monitors' reactions—stone-faced silence and crossed arms. What Mr. Watkins failed to find out was that the lunch monitors had met to discuss what had occurred, and they had prepared a list of possible ideas to improve the conditions in the cafeteria. Abigail Henson, the senior staff present, quietly folded the notes and put them back in her pocket, and they let the dean rant for a few minutes until he left. However, the damage was done. Ms. Henson voiced what the others were feeling: "I feel so disrespected."

We have all had times when our emotions got the best of us. One action that is vital is acknowledging when you're wrong. This is a demonstration of honesty. It doesn't necessarily wipe away what was said, but it does signal the start of rebuilding a bridge. Let's take each of these five facets of trust and look at common leadership behaviors that build or decrease trust (Figure 1.3).

FIGURE 1.3 CONVEYING AND DERAILING OUR TRUST

FACET OF TRUST	ACTIONS THAT CONVEY TRUST	ACTIONS THAT DERAIL TRUST
Benevolence	• Asking about another's well-being • Offering help when it is needed • Being patient with others and presuming positive intentions • Paying attention to the emotions of others • Exhibiting respect for every individual	• Ignoring difficulties people are experiencing (personal challenges don't belong in the workplace) • When someone challenges the wisdom of a decision, taking it as a personal affront; they're undermining your authority

FACET OF TRUST	ACTIONS THAT CONVEY TRUST	ACTIONS THAT DERAIL TRUST
Benevolence (continued)	• Being of service to others, even when there's no direct benefit to you • Celebrating the achievements of others	• Playing favorites • Always thinking about your own career first; being a leader is about gaining and holding on to power
Honesty	• Proving accurate data, even when it isn't favorable for you • Acknowledging when you are wrong • Admitting when you don't have the answer and vowing to find out more	• Taking credit for other people's work • Blaming others when something doesn't go well • Shading the truth so that you come out looking like a hero • Faking it when you don't know something
Reliability	• Honoring the commitments you have made • Following up with others about decisions that impact them • Following through with actions, not just words	• Making excuses when you don't deliver on commitments; you're busy, and everyone knows that • Keeping everyone guessing about what you'll do or say next
Openness	• Communicating with others to keep them informed • Disclosing your own concerns and uncertainties • Asking for the opinions and insights of others • Building personal connections with others	• Dominating the conversation; everyone needs to hear your ideas first • Asking for advice, but not actually using it • Scoffing at or dismissing other people's ideas • Gossiping
Competence	• Being clear and consistent on the purpose of the decisions and actions taken • Explaining your thought processes • Linking decisions and actions to the values and mission of the organization	• Making decisions alone; that's why you're the leader • Telling others what to do; you don't owe them an explanation

▶ Now imagine you are Mr. Watkins's supervisor. As dean of students, he requires mentoring, too. How might you advise him to repair his trust with the lunch staff?

BUILDING TRUST WHEN YOU'RE THE NEW PRINCIPAL

Trust is hard-won and easily lost. This is especially true when a principal is new to a school. The circumstances that led to the change in leadership are varied, to be sure. Perhaps you succeeded a principal who took on a new role within or outside of the district. Or perhaps the previous principal retired or left under a cloud of difficulties. The previous principal may have been a beloved figure (we worked with a school that had only four principals in 60 years—that's a tough act to follow). In any of those circumstances, building trust is at the top of the to-do list.

This takes time and effort, which is why most new leaders write 30-, 60-, and 90-day plans that include relational trust, among other tasks. It is useful to think about building trust at a new school as a series of stages, where trust becomes "thicker" and therefore less fragile over time (Bottery, 2005). For new and succeeding principals, these stages can be essential for building the kind of trust that is crucial among constituents. Northfield (2014) states that it begins with *role trust*, which is the expectation by a school community that the new leader has the credentials needed, and therefore knowledge, to ensure that the organization follows needed legal mandates, regulations, and governance requirements. Moreover, this first level of tacit trust assumes that the principal will act like a principal and the teacher will act like a teacher, with understood boundaries that keep the parties within the legal confines of their job descriptions. Should a situation arise that falls within the legal boundaries, teachers would be confident about how the new principal would respond. This is closely related to elements of competence, an important dimension of trustworthiness.

The second stage, *practice trust*, builds on the first. Not all situations that occur fall strictly within legal boundaries, so staff are also keeping an eye on how the new principal operates in action. As a simple example, how does the principal greet students and families? Is she out at the car drop-off area every morning to say hello? Or is he rarely out and about, spending more time in his office than in the hallways? There's no legal requirement that governs a principal's comportment. However, much of the practice trust gained (or not) is based on multiple observations over time as team members witness the actions of the new principal. There is a lot of impression making that is occurring. In order to reach this stage, staff members need to feel confident that they can predict how a principal will react in a given situation. Reliability, therefore, plays a role in practice trust.

This stage poses a potential pitfall. All four of us have worked or currently work in the field of university principal preparation, and too often we hear candidates say that they would devote the first six months of their new job to "listening" but not taking any action. But imagine the impatience of a staff who sees the new principal as passive and inactive. The opposite is equally problematic; the new principal who rushes in eager to adopt whatever (block scheduling, teacher clarity, integrated math, you name it) without bothering to learn about the organization's history risks trampling over team members' knowledge, skills, and beliefs. Development of practice trust requires a balance of making time to immerse oneself in learning about the school while ensuring that administrative tasks are completed and organizational learning continues.

Integrative trust is the third stage of trust development and is derived in part from the first two stages. The staff of the school are assured of the principal's ability to function within the legal guidelines and have witnessed a consistent level of action. Further, the principal's values and ethics are apparent. There is an intersection between integrative trust and benevolence, the belief that the leader has the long-term well-being of others in the organization in mind. For some principals, this is the stage is where trust stagnates. A lack of consistency and transparency and the conveyance of benevolence can prevent integrative trust from emerging.

The fourth stage, not reached by all, is *correlative trust*. This is evidenced when the principal and the staff have shared goals and values and work in tandem to realize ongoing and new initiatives. Is it possible that those Chicago schools that were successful in positively impacting reading and mathematics achievement had a higher degree of correlative trust? While Northfield presented these as stages, it is important to note that these are not static. The degree of trust can be gained and lost due to a single extraordinary event, or because of patterns over time (see Figure 1.4 for a summary).

FIGURE 1.4 STAGES OF TRUST

STAGES OF TRUST	DESCRIPTION OF THE LEVEL
Role trust	Staff members expect the principal to function according to the prescribed role and within the legal mandate of the position, including abiding by the laws, policies, and regulations that govern education and the position.
Practice trust	After observing the principal's practice and actions, staff members can predict how a principal will respond/act in a given situation.
Integrative trust	After observing/experiencing the actions of the principal in a multitude of situations, staff members are able to identify the underlying principles, values, and beliefs on which the principal chooses to act.
Correlative trust	Staff members understand and share the principal's values and beliefs such that they are able to function in a mutually respectful and supportive manner.

SOURCE: Northfield (2014, p. 412). Used with permission.

Ana Escobedo was appointed as the new principal of an elementary school in the district where she currently worked. Ms. Escobedo had been the principal of a smaller school for four years before receiving this assignment, when the principal she was succeeding, a beloved figure, announced her retirement. She began her appointment on July 1, where she had the opportunity to work with a few staff members over the summer. Teachers returned in late August, and Ms. Escobedo led a number of events, sometimes with other staff members, during the planning week. During small- and large-group conversations, she had a chance to share her vision and find out from others what their concerns were, as well as strengths. "I asked each person I spoke to if they could share one thing they are known for," Ms. Escobedo said. "It gave me some good insight into their personalities." She recognized that she was on her way to establishing initial role trust with her staff and now needed to do the same with students and families.

PAUSE AND PONDER

▶ What advice do you have for Ms. Escobedo about what she will want to accomplish during the first month of school? Keep practice trust in mind, as this is the next stage she is aspiring to reach.

PRACTICES TO STRENGTHEN TRUSTWORTHINESS

Your credibility as a leader of teams, departments, and schools begins and ends with your perceived trustworthiness. We don't get to say that we are trustworthy; it is determined by those around us. Trust is something that is always in play and, as such, is fluid. It is shaped by every interaction but gets thicker as you assemble a track record of benevolence, honesty, reliability, openness, and competence. Consider making these actions a part of your professional plan for developing and deepening your leadership skills:

Invest with intention. Trustworthiness isn't a static construct; therefore, you benefit from continuous investment. When in the role of a new leader, we're often quite conscious of how we establish trust. But it can be easy to let some of those practices fall away as we get busy with the tasks at hand. Keep in mind that trust evolves in phases, and role and practice trust shouldn't be seen as the final destination. Move your trustworthiness forward to build relational trust within your group. And if you've been a leader of a team for a while, reflect on what you did at the beginning of your tenure. Have you done anything like that in the last 30 days? If not, it's time to bring back some of those practices.

Notice when you are building and diminishing your own trust. Keep a log for a week to tally the times when you are building trust (e.g., following up, holding a confidence, keeping your emotions in check) and when you are diminishing trust (e.g., being late, not replying to a request, canceling plans, passing judgment on someone else). Your intention is to grow your own self-awareness.

Have the courage to ask others about trust. Identify a colleague who is credible to you and discuss the role of trustworthiness as an influence on your own credibility. Then ask the person if they would be willing to watch your interactions over the course of a week to note incidents when you appeared to build trust with others. If the person is willing, ask for feedback from them about your areas of strength and need as they relate to trust.

CONCLUSION

As humans, we rely on our ability to determine who is trustworthy and who isn't as a means of survival. While we aren't on the lookout for saber-toothed tigers anymore, we do tend to put our guard back up when we believe someone is not being truthful or is unreliable. We will return to the place this chapter began, which was the research conducted in Chicago Public Schools. Without question, all the educators, students, and family members were working hard to elevate learning. But there were some schools that were more advantaged than others because they had a higher degree of relational trust. They stood out because of four factors: mutual respect, personal regard, competence in core responsibilities, and personal integrity. These don't somehow just emerge in a school community. They are cultivated with intention. And a central tenet of leadership is this: walk the talk. It begins with us.

CHAPTER 2

....

COMPETENCE

The Language and Skills of Leaders

You've heard the phrase "leading by walking around," but maybe that should be changed to "leading by *talking* around." Much of the work of leaders is accomplished through conversation. In meetings, school hallways, and brief discussions with people throughout the day, we lead. In fact, one study estimated that oral communication makes up 70% of a principal's workday (Bredeson, 1987). Talk is the vehicle for how educational leadership is accomplished. It is the dominant channel for how we transmit our goodwill, our trustworthiness, and our expertise. There's a sobering statistic that represents the other side of the coin: superintendents of Texas school districts cited "fail to communicate or build positive relationships" as the most common reason principals were involuntarily separated from schools (Davila et al., 2012, p. 7). Stated more directly, trustworthiness and communication competence are essential skills leaders must master.

Before going further, we invite you to self-assess your competence as a leader. We encourage you to reflect on actions you have taken *in the last 30 days* to invest in your competence as a leader (see Figure 2.1).

FIGURE 2.1 COMPETENCE SELF-ASSESSMENT

COMPETENCE					
ITEM #	SURVEY ITEM	3 ALWAYS	2 SOMETIMES	1 RARELY	0 NEVER
1.	I invest in my own self-development and strive to stay current on research for effective teaching and leading.				
2.	I demonstrate strong instructional leadership through well-organized, purposeful conversations with teachers about evidence-based teaching and learning practices.				
3.	I strive to provide clarity on instructional practices that work best, and I provide feedback based on success criteria.				
4.	I prioritize time for daily classroom visits where I engage in conversations about teaching and learning with staff and students.				
5.	I drop in on PLC meetings to offer support and guidance to teams.				

COMPETENCE					
ITEM #	SURVEY ITEM	3 ALWAYS	2 SOMETIMES	1 RARELY	0 NEVER
6.	I seek and act on feedback from staff, students, and parents to improve the effectiveness of my leadership.				
Mean for Competence *(Total divided by 6)*					

REAL REFLECTION

Which of the indicators of competence are strengths for you?

Which of the indicators present growth opportunities?

What conclusions are you drawing about your perceived competence?

Whom can you enlist to support you in strengthening your competence and thus building your credibility?

THE RESEARCH ON COMPETENCE

The literature on leader competence comes in two strands: communication competence and skill competence. We'll take on the first strand before discussing the second. Trust and communication competence go hand in hand. In fact, a higher degree of trust between staff and leaders can result in more efficient communication as it "reduces the number of transactions among employees necessary to complete tasks" (Sutherland & Yoshida, 2015, p. 1039). When trust is solid, things get done faster and better.

Keeping in mind that the majority of a principal's workday is devoted to oral communication, it is somewhat surprising that the specific talk moves used by leaders aren't more thoroughly discussed. While the educational leadership research is replete with advice about the importance of "open communication," less has been developed on what this actually looks and sounds like. One study, a comparison of a measure of trust between principals and teachers and a measure of the principal's oral competence, found that coordination of attentiveness was the primary factor (Sutherland & Yoshida, 2021). The research showed that a principal's attention to sharing air time with the teacher (not dominating the space), sustaining the interaction to keep the discussion going, and managing interruptions proved to be important contributors to trust.

The second strand is skill competence, which is the perception that a leader has the requisite knowledge and implements it to improve conditions. This is accomplished not by displaying framed degrees in your office but rather by putting skills into action. Having said that, you can't fully separate communication from skills; verbal and written language is central to action. Effective leaders use three types of leader speech: direction-giving language, empathetic language, and meaning-making language to spark action, build relationships, and communicate the reasoning behind decisions (Sullivan, 1988). Together, these three speech types constitute motivating language theory (MLT), a communication theory about how leaders use talk to improve an organization. In their review of MLT, Holmes and Parker (2018, pp. 437–438) offer examples of the use of each of these speech types in schools:

- **Direction-giving language** clarifies and reduces uncertainty, focuses teachers on goals and objectives, increases teacher and staff knowledge and information, and provides feedback and rewards. Principals use direction-giving language, for example, during post-observation conversations with teachers to clarify teaching expectations, provide suggestions for improvement, and deliver rewarding instructional feedback.

- **Empathetic language** values teachers and staff as human beings, not objects; emphasizes concern and consideration; reinforces trust; influences effort through encouragement and praise; and guides individual professional development. Principals use empathetic language, for instance, in the delegation of professional development to instructional coaches and their expressions of support, encouragement, praise, and concern for job satisfaction during planning and debriefing sessions with them.

- **Meaning-making language** assists teachers in finding meaning at work; assists school employees in understanding the school culture (especially the unwritten cultural rules); supports personal employee vision alignment with school/district vision; increases teacher effectiveness during change and induction periods; and shows appreciation for successful school employee efforts. Principals use meaning-making language, for example, during staff meetings to recognize exemplary teacher behavior as a means to reinforce appropriate school culture behaviors as well as during leadership team meetings describing the behaviors of struggling teachers along with discussing methods of support and intervention for them.

In their review of the research on motivating language usage by principals, Holmes and Parker noted that the skilled use of these speech types accomplishes three important goals linked to credibility: (1) establishing goodwill (benevolence) (2) trustworthiness, and (3) competence. This last feature of motivational language is crucial for instructional leadership; when "teachers believe the administrator knows little about pedagogy [expertness and knowledge]; ... the principal's suggestions [leadership ability] for improving teaching performance are ignored" (2018, p. 441).

From the standpoint of teachers, much of an administrator's skill competence is demonstrated in the use of motivational language but is best translated as working conditions. Leaders are variously charged with overseeing and managing operations, resource allocation, curricular decisions, and supports. Working conditions are defined as teacher time use, physical environment, teacher empowerment/school leadership, and professional development (Burkhauser, 2017).

Using a large data set from North Carolina, Burkhauser examined relationships between a measure of teacher empowerment and their reports on their working conditions. Not surprisingly, in schools where good working conditions attributable to the principal existed, teacher turnover was low. In schools where principal-attributed working conditions were poor, teacher turnover was high. Recommendations from the researchers to districts included assessing teachers' perceptions of working conditions and strengthening the skills and communication competence of principals.

COMPETENCE FOR PROVIDING AND RECEIVING FEEDBACK

The ability to provide feedback to others depends on a measure of communication competence. Turning to the world of business, consider that a study of the role of communication credibility for 477 full-time employees found that trustworthiness, goodwill (benevolence), and the ability to communicate with clarity were essential for the feedback to "stick" (Kingsley Westerman et al., 2018). Perhaps of most interest (and a segue into the second kind of competence) was that the source credibility was a mediating factor. In other words, the skill competence of the supervisor played a deciding role in whether the feedback was accepted or not.

No doubt you have used the phrase "consider the source" when you have heard something you do not accept. That's what source credibility is. When receiving feedback, one of the factors the recipient weighs, whether a student or a staff member, is the degree to which they believe the provider has the expert knowledge to give it. If the recipient decides the provider does not have that knowledge, the feedback is dismissed. If the recipient decides the provider has the expertise, the likelihood that the feedback with be accepted is increased. We'll discuss source credibility in more detail in Chapter 3, but for now, suffice to say that source credibility is a conceptual bridge between communication competence and skill competence.

It's important to state that, left to our own tendencies, we'll stay within our comfort zone. Former English teachers who are now leaders tend to spend more time in English classrooms, while an administrator with credentials in physical education might give more attention to the athletics program.

Secondary mathematics teachers and special education teachers routinely report receiving less instructional guidance from administrators who feel that they aren't experts and therefore avoid getting more involved. But as leaders, it is essential for us to be aware of where our knowledge gaps lie and take steps to improve our knowledge.

No matter how competent we are in terms of credentials and licensure, we can't be experts to all people in every aspect of their jobs. Christopher Milton, principal of a busy elementary school, was aware of this when he met with the transportation director of his district. Mr. Milton's school was located in an urban area, on a corner of two streets with high traffic and no shoulders. There was metered parking on the streets, and families picking up and dropping off students presented a backup onto the city streets. Recently, police started ticketing cars idling in line on the public streets for blocking traffic.

The elementary principal knew he was not a traffic and safety expert, but he did have knowledge of the demands families face before and after school. In preparation for the meeting, he spoke with several families who transported their children to and from school. In addition, he met with the crossing guards who worked the morning and afternoon shifts to gain their perspectives. In addition, he familiarized himself with the municipal regulations concerning traffic control.

The transportation director, Alberto Gomez, started the meeting by expressing his frustration about the situation. He began to lecture Mr. Milton about the problems he was facing: "I got another phone call from the chief [of police] yesterday. This is not what I need." However, Mr. Milton was able to change the tenor of the discussion pretty rapidly when he shared with the director the fact-finding he had completed prior to the meeting. After presenting, Mr. Milton said, "I think we can arrive at a good solution for all involved. You've definitely got the expertise about how this situation can be improved. You redesigned the drop-off and pick-up procedures for Lincoln Elementary, right? The principal there told me how much of an improvement it has been. I'd like to run some ideas by you so we can figure this out."

▶ Mr. Milton set about building his knowledge so he could provide good feedback in his meeting with the transportation director. How do you build expertise to give and receive good feedback in situations where you don't have as much existing knowledge?

COMPETENCE IN CONFLICT MANAGEMENT

Conflict management requires a high degree of communication and skill competence. All school organizations have conflict, and leaders must manage how conflict is addressed and managed within and across teams. Think about it this way—much of the talk that occurs between leaders and staff are low-level negotiations that seek to manage conflict. Blake and Moulton (1964) sought to define conflict as being something more than two extremes: competing, meaning that there is a winner and a loser; or avoiding, in hopes that the conflict will somehow resolve itself. They expanded the continuum to include five styles, which Shell, writing in the *Negotiation Journal* further defined:

- **Competing orientation:** A dominant, high concern for the self's goals and associated desire to limit the other's results

- **Collaborating orientation:** A balanced, high level of concern for self's and other's goals and results

- **Compromising orientation:** A balanced, moderate level of concern for both self and the other

- **Accommodating orientation:** A dominant, high concern for the other's goals without much concern for the self

- **Avoiding orientation:** A disinclination toward placing the self in conflict with others to pursue any goals at all (Shell, 2001, p. 159)

Disagreement is a part of any team, and a degree of disagreement is necessary to innovate and engage in meaningful change. However, conflict can be more destructive. Many conflicts within organizations have root causes related to differences in values, goals, and tasks (Van De Vliert, 1998), and these underlying root causes of conflict are exacerbated by circumstances influenced by the leader, including

- **Problems in communication,** including a lack of openness, lack of responsiveness, and withholding information

- **Role ambiguity** through lack of clarity about job responsibilities

- **Incompatible goals** that prevent another goal from being achieved

- **Conflict of interest** when limited resources require groups to fight for their own share

- **Differences in values** due to lack of consensus building within or across teams (Saiti, 2014)

Several studies have held that a leader's communication and skill competence can be correlated to the amount of conflict within a school organization (Üstüner & Kiş, 2014) and how that conflict is managed (Uzun & Ayik, 2017). This last study found that principals who used the conflict management styles of avoidance (ignoring the conflict) or accommodating (placing more value on the other person's perspective than on your own) had more conflict within the school. You may find it surprising that an accommodating style of conflict management doesn't yield good results. In truth, it undermines perceptions of the skill competence of the leader, who is seen as self-sacrificing and weak. The result is that this approach undermines confidence in the leader and can build resentment. Therefore, it comes as little surprise that these researchers reported that current conflicts handled using an accommodating or avoiding style served as a catalyst for future problems.

Kaitlin Grant was a vice principal of a large high school, and as part of her job duties, she oversaw the mathematics and science departments at the school. All the department heads met for their monthly debriefing, the latest of which Ms. Grant was not able to attend due to a scheduling conflict. She learned that a conflict arose during the meeting when Hal Green, the mathematics chair, reportedly said, "The science team isn't pulling their weight. Look at our latest math scores [on the state assessment]. We can only do so much. Kids aren't getting the necessary application practice they need in science and it's holding them back." Lisbeth Ramirez, the science department chair, was waiting at the vice principal's office door the following morning: "I've had it with Hal and the way he undercuts the science department," she told Ms. Grant. "I've tried to talk with him privately about his behavior in our chairs meetings, and I'm not getting anywhere. You need to do something to make him stop. If you don't, I will be stepping down as chair and applying for a transfer to another school."

Ms. Grant knew that she needed to intervene, but she also needed to learn more about the backstory. A challenge for leaders is that they often must respond quickly to situations that are ill-defined (Robinson et al., 2021). Knowing that a "he said/she said" fact-finding mission would yield little useful information for managing this conflict, Ms. Grant used an approach that she learned about in a conflict management course offered by her state administrators association, defined by Robinson and colleagues (2021). She spoke separately to Ms. Ramirez and Mr. Green to learn more and made notes to herself to prepare (see Figure 2.2).

FIGURE 2.2 MS. GRANT'S NOTES

STAGE OF PROBLEM SOLVING	MS. RAMIREZ'S BELIEFS	MR. GREEN'S BELIEFS
Problem description beliefs	Mr. Green publicly criticized her team.	Math scores have declined for the last two years.

STAGE OF PROBLEM SOLVING	MS. RAMIREZ'S BELIEFS	MR. GREEN'S BELIEFS
Problem description beliefs (continued)	Public criticism is harmful.	Discussions about interdisciplinary approaches for science and math have gone nowhere.
	We have a strong science program, and using an interdisciplinary approach might dilute it.	Ms. Ramirez is blocking innovation.
Problem explanation beliefs	Mr. Green wants to be the boss of everything.	Ms. Ramirez doesn't like change.
	I haven't been effective in sharing my concerns with Mr. Green.	I have not been effective in explaining the benefits of an interdisciplinary plan.
Problem solution beliefs	Mr. Green should talk to me about his concerns before the meeting.	Ms. Ramirez should give this a try. Nothing else has worked to change the math scores.
	Mr. Green should be looking more closely at what effective math instruction looks like and start from there.	

Using the notes she had gathered from individual conversations with each of them, the vice principal felt equipped to broker a solution. She believed, on review, that Mr. Green and Ms. Ramirez were locked in a competing orientation. Her goal was to move them to a collaborating orientation. She shared with them the concerns each had raised, using a version of the notes she had gathered to print for them so she could refer them to each other's beliefs when the discussion veered off track. They mutually agreed that Mr. Green and Ms. Ramirez would jointly propose an interdisciplinary pilot for the next school year and identify two teachers who wanted to explore this option. They also agreed they would monitor progress through the development of some common formative assessment items. Most importantly, Mr. Green conceded that public criticism was harmful, while Ms. Ramirez agreed that her stonewalling had contributed to Mr. Green's frustration.

LEADERSHIP PRACTICES THAT CONVEY AND DERAIL COMPETENCE

Perceptions of competence, as with every dimension of leader credibility, are in the eye of the beholder. While we don't get to decide that we are competent, we can be mindful of the every-day actions we do (and don't do) that can either convey or derail our communication and skill competence. Take a look at Figure 2.3. What do you do frequently and infrequently?

FIGURE 2.3 CONVEYING AND DERAILING OUR COMPETENCE

FACET OF COMPETENCE	ACTIONS THAT CONVEY COMPETENCE	ACTIONS THAT DERAIL COMPETENCE
Communication	• When directing staff, sharing your decision-making process and rationale	• Giving directions and expecting people to hop to it; that's why you're the boss
	• Acknowledging the work and accomplishments of others	• Overlooking the efforts of others
	• Linking progress and problems to the values of the organization; these are opportunities for climate building	• Stating directives using self-deflecting language (e.g., "Central office said we have to do this")
	• Using every opportunity to interact regularly with staff; this keeps little problems from getting bigger	• Spending the majority of your time in your office; those emails need to get answered!
	• Communicating primarily through talk	• Communicating primarily through email

FACET OF COMPETENCE	ACTIONS THAT CONVEY COMPETENCE	ACTIONS THAT DERAIL COMPETENCE
Skill	• When you don't know something, saying, "Let's find out together" or "I'll learn more about that and follow up with you"	• When you don't know something, saying, "That's not my area. Ask ____."
	• When conflict arises, learning about the perspectives and beliefs of each party to better equip yourself for facilitation	• At the first whiff of conflict, avoiding it altogether and hoping someone else manages it
	• When you are a direct party to the conflict, working through what you believe the other person would say about the description, explanation, and possible solution to a problem	• At the first whiff of conflict, exercising your authority to squelch it • At the first whiff of conflict, doing whatever you can to placate people so the issue will go away
	• Paying attention to the work conditions of the staff to proactively address challenges	• Viewing work conditions as "fine"; the staff is lucky to have jobs

PAUSE AND PONDER

▶ Reflect on an example of a highly competent leader from your own career. How did that person display their communication competence? Their skill competence?

COMPETENCE AND THE CHALLENGE OF THE INTERNAL APPOINTMENT

Many leaders move into a position through internal appointment within the same school, from teacher to department chair or instructional coach; from dean to assistant principal;

or from assistant principal to principal. Unlike leaders who move from one school to another, these leaders face unique obstacles regarding their perceived competence in their new roles. Dominant among these challenges is that the role change resulted in tension, especially negative behaviors and attitudes, from colleagues, much of it related to questioning the leader's qualifications for the new position, something those transferring from other schools do not face to the same degree. Some of these perceptions are internalized, and a challenge for those who have been internally promoted to a new leadership role is that "some start doubting their competence, their old anxieties resurface, and they even freeze" (Jaca, 2021, p. 246).

If you are a current leader, be on the lookout for internally promoted candidates and know that they will benefit greatly from your guidance and support as they step into their new roles. Principal supervisors should be especially alert to these circumstances, as internally promoted principals do not have a mentor to turn to on the site. Assistant principal Rachelle Kamaka met regularly with the department chairs at the middle school where she worked and was especially sensitive to this issue for new chairs. Tim Hayashi was the new chair of the social studies department, having been a faculty member at the school for seven years. However, he only taught sixth grade during that time. He was getting pushback from his former colleagues, especially those who taught Grades 7 and 8, because he hadn't taught those grade levels in the past.

Ms. Kamaka had witnessed some of the difficulties the new department chair encountered. Although providing feedback about instruction and curriculum was in his job description, some teachers were resistant. Knowing this to be the case, Ms. Kamaka offered to go on learning walks with Mr. Hayashi to sharpen his eye (Fisher, Frey, Almarode, Flories, & Nagel, 2019). Although she didn't state it directly, the assistant principal was aware that it was an opportunity to share her competence publicly so that the other teachers in the department would witness the positive regard she had for his skills.

▶ What do you think of Ms. Kamaka's approach? Do you have additional suggestions for how to support an internally promoted staff member facing questions about his competence?

PRACTICES TO STRENGTHEN COMPETENCE

Your competence as a leader of teams, schools, or units is more than the sum of your previous experiences. Too often, quite frankly, people are placed into leadership roles by virtue of their credentials and licensure. But the evidence on leader competence goes beyond those details. It is massively linked to one's communication competence, just as verbal and written communication should be more than a list of directives. It must include language that is motivating, especially to continue to build trust and link to the organization's values. The skill competence is also important, but it doesn't start with "When I was a fourth-grade teacher, I . . .". Quite frankly, that wears thin pretty quickly. The skills you possess go beyond content knowledge and are evidenced in the ways you negotiate, manage conflict, and give and receive feedback. Consider making these actions a part of your professional plan for developing and deepening your leadership skills.

Learn more about the language of leadership by noting its use by those you admire. Effective leaders have their own style, but underneath is a common thread of leader speech types: giving direction, engaging in empathetic language, and meaning for others. Take note of these talk moves used by leaders you look up to, as their style can provide insight into how they accomplish things. It can also free you from the self-defeating internal dialogue that goes something like "If only I was more like ____."

Bring conflict management training to your team. It's not just for those in highly litigious positions, like the special education director. As leaders, we manage conflict all the time. Teacher-leaders often talk about the fact (rightly so) that they didn't get any training to be a team leader. Your local or state organization may be a great source for this kind of professional development.

Sharpen your feedback skills. Feedback received (not given) advances learning. We also know that feedback is mediated by the relationship that the two people have. When preparing for providing feedback to a staff member, consider the relationship you have with that person. In addition, model the practice of seeking feedback by regularly checking in with others you work with to solicit feedback from them.

CONCLUSION

Educators rely on leaders to build and maintain conditions for them to perform at their highest level. A leader who is perceived as lacking competence creates fear and hesitancy in others who may be unsure whether that person is going to lead them off a cliff. Competence is conveyed through the talk moves we use every day. Keep in mind the statistic we shared with you at the beginning of this chapter: 70% of a principal's day is spent talking. So the real question is, how can you elevate that talk to build competence and trust? And what are the actions that need to occur in order to align the talk with the walk?

CHAPTER 3

·····························

DYNAMISM

Passion, Excitement, and
Self-Confidence to
Build Credibility

Before we begin our discussion on dynamism, take a few minutes to respond to the self-assessment in Figure 3.1, which reflects the main ideas and elements of becoming a dynamic leader. This information can help you focus on the content that matters most to you as you read through the chapter.

FIGURE 3.1 DYNAMISM SELF-ASSESSMENT
···

DYNAMISM					
ITEM #	SURVEY ITEM	3 ALWAYS	2 SOMETIMES	1 RARELY	0 NEVER
1.	I am excited about the potential of my school to achieve great things and I effectively communicate this belief.				

(Continued)

(Continued)

DYNAMISM					
ITEM #	SURVEY ITEM	3 ALWAYS	2 SOMETIMES	1 RARELY	0 NEVER
2.	I enjoy engaging fully with my staff in professional learning, staff meetings, and other school events.				
3.	I am intentional about speaking with passion and excitement about the future possibilities for our school.				
4.	When appropriate, I use personal stories, relevant and interesting videos, pictures, slide presentations, articles, etc., to make messages come alive for all team members.				
5.	I seek and use feedback on how my staff perceives my levels of self-confidence and competence.				
Mean for Dynamism (Total divided by 5)					

Which of the indicators of dynamism are strengths for you?

Which of the indicators present growth opportunities?

What conclusions are you drawing about your dynamism?

Whom can you enlist to support you in strengthening your dynamism and thus building your credibility?

Dynamism is often described as a leader's perceived confidence, activity, and assertiveness. Dynamic leaders communicate confidence, inspire others to work harder, and make sacrifices for the group (including working hard themselves). According to renowned leadership researchers and professors Kouzes and Posner (2012), people admire and respect leaders who are dynamic, uplifting, enthusiastic, positive, and optimistic. Kouzes and Posner make this claim based on research, spanning more than 30 years, investigating what people expect from their leaders. The study resulted in a list of 225 values, characteristics, and traits that participants believed were crucial for effective leadership. The team of researchers culled the list from 225 factors to 15 categories of the most frequent responses. The top qualities appear below in order of response:

1. Integrity (includes *truthful, trustworthiness, character,* and *convictions*)

2. Competence (includes *capable, productive,* and *efficient*)

3. Leadership (includes *inspiring, visionary, decisive,* and *direction*)

Over the three decades Kouzes and Posner have been collecting data, the results have remained quite consistent over time, across the globe, and spanning demographic groups including age, gender, ethnicity, discipline, organizational level, and industry. It seems that workers at any level, in any business, in any part of the world, are clear about the leadership qualities that influence their decisions to support and engage in the work their leader proposes. In short, the qualities listed above are those that determine workers' motivation to follow their leaders.

From this empirical data, the researchers created a list of crucial leadership attributes that determine a leader's credibility with the workforce:

1. Honesty

2. Forward looking

3. Inspiring

4. Competent

You have been reading about several of these attributes in the prior chapters. In this chapter, we focus on dynamism, which includes a leader's ability to inspire, demonstrate passion, and lead with confidence to be believable.

Let's start with an example. Arianna Jimenez was an elementary school principal serving a diverse student population just outside of Washington, D.C. The students and families were hard hit by COVID-19 and virtual learning. Students returned to school with unfinished learning that needed to be addressed. Ms. Jimenez recognized that what teachers needed from her was inspiration, passion, and a "can-do" approach to the work. She shared the data, but more importantly, she clearly and passionately expressed her confidence in teachers' abilities, her commitment to the children they serve, and her ideas for going forward. Notably, she also asked for feedback and input on how they would move the school forward as a team and emphasized that the students were behind not for a lack of ability but rather for a lack of opportunity to learn with qualified, committed teachers. As a result, Ms. Jimenez bolstered her credibility with her staff and the families by being transparent, competent, and dynamic in her approach to this unprecedented challenge in schools.

How do you think Ms. Jimenez's staff responded? They responded in kind. They developed their own can-do approach, working together as a team. In doing so, they began to strategically chip away at the learning gaps. The research shows that leaders who demonstrate dynamism, are passionate, committed, and all-in on the work elicit the same response from their teams. Holmes et al. (2021) analyzed the motivating language used by superintendents on the perceived job satisfaction and competence of their principals. It should come as little surprise that there was a reciprocal relationship between the two: principals reported higher levels of satisfaction when superintendents used motivating language that sought to build trust, competence, and goodwill. In doing so, principals perceived their superintendents as being credible and more clearly understood the links between words and actions.

As Lassiter (2017) noted, leaders (and teachers, for that matter) get what they give. If you project passion, excitement, and a sense of urgency for teaching and learning, the school community will mirror the same right back to you. They will be excited, engaged, and ready to learn and work on something important. But if you project indifference, insecurity, and a lack of preparation, or if you demonstrate a lackadaisical attitude toward the work ahead, those attitudes and behaviors will be projected right back to you. Your teams will become unconcerned, unengaged, and uninterested in the important work you are advocating, which will contribute to their underperformance down the road.

DYNAMISM AND SELF-CONFIDENCE

At this point, you might be thinking that being a dynamic leader sounds great and you are on board with why it matters to your credibility, but you're not sure if you have the self-confidence to pull it off. Your thinking is spot-on, as self-confidence is a required element of dynamic leadership and thus your credibility.

Folkman and his colleague Zenger examined the influence of confidence on overall leadership effectiveness (Folkman, 2019). Their data confirm that self-confidence is a beneficial trait for leaders. More specifically, their study showed that for 90% of the 1,500 plus leaders in the study, increasing leadership competence was strongly connected with increasing confidence. However, in 10% of the cases when high self-confidence preceded competence, it had a damaging impact because these leaders wrongly assumed they were competent, but their results and the feedback from others did not validate their assumptions. The result is damaging to leader credibility because staff see you as being super confident without knowing what you are talking about. This unfortunate situation reinforces the value of leaders seeking and using regular feedback from staff to determine how they perceive you and whether they view you as a credible leader.

Additionally, in the areas of displaying integrity, honesty, and relationship building, these "non-improvers" showed a decreased level of effectiveness with increased confidence. Therefore, exhibiting overconfidence before developing competence in the job significantly impedes the building of leadership credibility.

PAUSE AND PONDER

▶ Have you experienced working with a leader whose confidence exceeded their competence? How did staff members feel about this leader? Was this leader viewed as credible?

Now, the 90% of leaders with higher ratings in self-confidence also rated significantly more positively on the following six leadership traits:

1. **Being a champion.** High-confidence leaders were more willing to be a champion for projects or programs.

2. **Having the courage to change.** High-confidence leaders were rated as being more courageous and willing to make bold changes. They were quick to spot problems and recognized the need to change early.

3. **Having more energy and enthusiasm.** Leaders with high self-confidence were evaluated as having more energy

and the ability to energize others. They were also more enthusiastic.

4. **Willing to challenge.** High-confidence leaders were more likely to challenge standard approaches and encourage others to find new, more innovative ways to do work.

5. **Inspiring.** High-confidence leaders were rated as being more inspiring. They had the ability to motivate others, and their approach was more *pull* than *push*.

6. **Representing the group.** The high-confidence leaders were rated significantly higher on their ability to represent their group to other groups or to customers. (Folkman, 2019. From Forbes. © 2019 Forbes. All rights reserved. Used under license.)

Conversely, when a leader's self-confidence became overconfidence, especially without high competence, negative traits tended to emerge:

1. **Lack of trust.** Being overconfident can diminish trust from others.

2. **Arrogance.** Often the overconfident will resist feedback and personal change.

3. **Damaged relationships.** Often the overconfident will not notice or be concerned with others.

4. **Honesty and integrity.** The overconfident fail to honor their commitments and are poor role models. (Folkman, 2019. From Forbes. © 2019 Forbes. All rights reserved. Used under license.)

PAUSE AND PONDER

▶ Take a moment to think about the results of these studies. Was there something you learned that supported your thinking? What was it? Did you learn something new that has influenced your current thinking? What was that? Did you read something that has inspired you to start planning an action or a next step? What was that?

In our experience in schools, leaders, especially new leaders, do not suffer from overconfidence. Rather, they most typically exhibit a lack of confidence in leading their schools or teams. To support the development of necessary self-confidence to build dynamism and overall credibility, we believe in the power of deliberate practice, first posited by Anders Ericsson and colleagues in 1993. Deliberate practice allows leaders to focus on one or two essential skills at a time, seeking feedback and adjusting as they learn. We believe that this is much more effective in building self-confidence than pointing out every flaw or mistake a leader makes during their development.

If you suspect that you possess an overconfidence without the necessary competence, Folkman and Zenger's overconfidence test (Folkman, 2019) can generate some helpful information for your deliberate practice and overall leadership growth.

Overconfidence Test

Ask staff members to anonymously respond to the following questions:

1. Am I trusted by others?

2. Do I ask others for candid feedback on what I can do to improve?

3. When I ask for feedback, do I make a real effort to change?

4. Am I in touch with the issues and concerns of others?

5. Am I balancing getting results with the needs and concerns of others?

6. Do I follow through on commitments and keep promises?

7. Am I a role model? (Folkman, 2019. From Forbes. © 2019 Forbes. All rights reserved. Used under license.)

Accept the data: the good, the bad, and the ugly. Consider charting or graphing the data to illustrate your growth over time. Line or bar graphs or pie charts will help you analyze the data objectively to determine how your workforce perceives your confidence or overconfidence. It may also be helpful to seek out a trusted colleague or mentor to assist in determining the next steps.

A second strategy for strengthening self-confidence is keeping your worries in perspective. Worrying constantly will not help you override fear, and it will impede your ability to reflect and change. Worrying drains valuable energy, takes away needed focus, causes fatigue and stress, and steals joy. Worrying is a confidence killer, but it can and should be deliberately controlled (Lassiter, 2017). Make a list of the things you have worried most about recently. Keep these worries in mind as you consider the research that follows.

Researchers asked a group of people to identify what worried them and tracked their worries over time. The important results are presented in Figure 3.2.

FIGURE 3.2   RESEARCH ON WHAT PEOPLE WORRY ABOUT

40%	of the worries concerned things that never actually happened
30%	of the worries concerned things from the past that could neither be changed nor otherwise influenced
12%	of the worries were needless worries about health
10%	of the worries were petty worries about unimportant things
8%	of the worries concerned anything substantial
And half of the substantial issues 4%	worries about substantial things that could be controlled or changed

SOURCE: Cottrell and Harvey (2004, p. 82).

PAUSE AND PONDER

▶ Did any of the worries you listed show up in the chart? Could the time you spent worrying have been spent on more productive endeavors? Is the amount of time you spend worrying impeding your ability to become a dynamic, confident leader?

Highly effective leaders have worries just like the rest of us, but they deliberately refuse to waste their energy stressing over things over which they have no control. Rather, they direct their energy and attention to factors they can control, and they do so with passion, enthusiasm, and determination. Research shows that the best antidote for worry is purposeful action. Engaging in actions that make a difference for others and fearlessly focusing on the work that matters most can help you keep your worries at bay and build the confidence you need to make important decisions for school improvement (Lassiter, 2017).

So, the next time you find yourself unable to focus or lacking energy and motivation due to worrying, ask yourself if your worries fall into one of the categories listed. Force yourself to keep things in perspective by understanding that 96% of the things you worry about will not happen, are out of your control, are needless, or are really unimportant in the big picture.

DYNAMISM AND SOURCE CREDIBILITY

Source credibility, simply put, is the reliability and accuracy of sources of information, whether they be print/text, images, video, or speeches from individuals. Leaders in all fields choose and use a variety of sources every day to validate their messages, implement new programs, make decisions and create mission and vision statements. But what happens to a leader's credibility if the sources they choose turn out to be inaccurate, unreliable, or just plain false? What if a leader passionately and enthusiastically presents a change idea or personal vision for an organization and the information they use to support their message is unsubstantiated? The answer is that they will lose the trust, respect, and engagement of their workforce and will likely struggle mightily to get it back. That is why we are including this important topic in a book about credibility.

Consider George Henderson. He was the director of curriculum and instruction in a small rural school district in Florida. Not having a huge budget to work with, Mr. Henderson was on the hunt for an assessment program that would enable teachers to create and score their own formative assessments.

He met a consultant at a conference who struck up a conversation with him, and Mr. Henderson learned that this man had created a program that would do exactly what Mr. Henderson was looking for. This program was research-based, used vetted scoring processes, and was offered at a price Mr. Henderson's district could afford. The consultant agreed to provide initial training and then quarterly coaching for staff. Mr. Henderson was ecstatic.

Over the summer, contracts were signed, and the rollout and subsequent training dates were put on the school calendar. Mr. Henderson shared the information with the administrators at their summer retreat, and the consultant conducted a brief demonstration of how the program worked. Everyone was very excited after listening to the consultant's engaging presentation.

When teachers returned in August, they learned about the new assessment tool and looked forward to the workshop on how to use it. The first workshop with elementary teachers went well. Mr. Henderson was very pleased, and the teachers enjoyed the presentation style of the consultant. Then the secondary sessions began, and so did the problems. The software kept freezing. The teachers noticed accuracy issues with the scoring mechanism and began to ask questions that seemed to stump the consultant. One of the teachers then researched the consultant's name and company and found that there were many school districts that had experienced issues with the program and the consultant. The teachers wondered why Mr. Henderson had not discovered the issues prior to signing a contract and spending the district's limited budget on something that was known to have so many flaws. Mr. Henderson had to answer for his failure to properly investigate the credibility of this source to both the superintendent and the school board. He had lost the trust of the teaching staff and his competence as a school leader was compromised. If Mr. Henderson had been aware of the importance of source credibility, he could have avoided this incredibly stressful and embarrassing situation.

We live in a time of information overload, fake news, and false media that force leaders to become more discerning about the sources they use to support their agendas. A misstep or mistake around source credibility can have far-reaching implications for leaders. Earning trust and building credibility takes time and consistent effort, and a single misstep or misjudgment can bring it all to a sudden end. Credible leaders are believed and trusted to make sound decisions using reliable sources for the good of all in the organization. Followers are confident in their judgment, respond favorably to requests, and more easily accept changes proposed by the leader. The opposite is true in organizations where the leader is deemed not credible by the workforce.

To maintain your credibility, you must seek sources that are credible, accurate, unbiased, and complete. There are three criteria that communications experts suggest we use to identify sources with these qualities. Interestingly, these criteria are similar to those we use to identify credible leaders. The three criteria follow:

1. Expertise

2. Trustworthiness

3. Dynamism

First, does the source have expertise? Examine the source's experience, knowledge, and skill that sets them beyond others in the field. Narrow expertise is usually more reliable than broad or general expertise, and relevant expertise is essential when using a source to support an initiative. Avoid choosing sources that have broad appeal but lack firsthand knowledge or relevant and specific expertise in the field. Remember, expertise is developed by doing the work and understanding the field as it is today, not 20 years ago. And fancy titles and boisterous claims do not make an expert.

Second, is the source trustworthy? To determine if a source is trustworthy, look at their work history, results, affiliations, associations, and motives. Examine their track record and look for consistency in their printed works, speeches, and workshops. Scrutinize their transparency about their research, program effectiveness, theories, and the like. Judge the quality of the sources they have used to develop their work; recognize that expertise alone does not mean the source is trustworthy. Oftentimes, we can be unduly influenced by the knowledge and expertise of a source and deem them trustworthy as a result. This blind trust gives a source the ability to mislead or misinform, motivated by a hidden bias, purpose, or agenda.

Third, does the source possess dynamism? As you listen to or read the works of this source, do you feel their sense of passion for the work? A source with dynamism is adept at conveying their love for the work and joy in sharing it with others. Sources with dynamism can draw listeners and/or readers into their message, which results in follower confidence in the source. Dynamism has a significant impact on the sources leaders deem credible. In fact, no matter how trustworthy or knowledgeable a source may be, we won't pay attention to them if their presentation of the material is boring, irrelevant, or unengaging.

Therefore, leaders must be disciplined when determining the credibility of selected sources by using all three of the criteria as a filter for their decisions. Putting too much weight on one criterion over the other two will lead to mistakes. Below is a list of red flags that suggest a source may not be credible:

- The source uses unnamed sources and does not readily share their sources or research.

- The source uses language that includes absolutes like *always, never, all,* and *every.* There are always outliers or exceptions.

- The source does not openly discuss or share their methodologies for analysis or research.

- The source is not willing or able to provide citations for quotes or full text from where quotes have been taken.

- The source fails to acknowledge both sides of an issue or theory. They do not acknowledge potential flaws or limitations in their work.

▶ To what extent have you and/or the other leaders in your district considered source credibility as an important aspect of your leadership credibility? Have you experienced situations like the one Mr. Henderson found himself in? How might you make source credibility a part of your regular process when choosing people or materials for your work?

Evaluating sources in a "post-truth" world is sadly a necessity in these times. We are suggesting that it might be beneficial to take the extra step to source check any research you plan to use in faculty meetings or in presentations. Or, as in the case of Mr. Henderson from Florida, do your homework on consultants and programs you plan to use, beyond the literature provided to you from the source. Asking for evidence of impact and checking on the evidence can save frustrations later and protect your hard-earned credibility in the school community.

Finally, source credibility may not be something you have thought about before, but in this age of information overload and rampant misinformation, leaders must carefully analyze the sources they choose to use as cornerstones for their agendas. You must be able to present your thoughts confidently and passionately, supported by credible sources and people, to make an impact on the hearts and minds of your staff. No leader wants to defend or explain why they failed to vet a particular source, research report, or speaker. The work of becoming a credible leader is too hard and takes too long to have it damaged by making uninformed source choices.

▶ How might you use the tools and information provided on source credibility to avoid having your decisions brought into question regarding the information you bring to schools or teams you lead?

LEADERSHIP PRACTICES THAT CONVEY AND DERAIL DYNAMISM

Who decides if a leader is passionate or dynamic? The short answer is everyone except the leader in question. Based on personal interactions, all humans who have contact with you will have perceptions about your passion for the work, and these perceptions influence your credibility with everyone in the school community. As was stated in Chapter 2, leader credibility is in the eye of the beholder. We are not the determiners of our own dynamism, competence, or trustworthiness; however, we can develop an awareness of the practices that convey these qualities and then intentionally demonstrate them with every opportunity. We must also be mindful of the behaviors that can derail our efforts and avoid them. Take a look at the chart in Figure 3.3. What do you do frequently and infrequently?

FIGURE 3.3 CONVEYING AND DERAILING OUR DYNAMISM

FACET OF DYNAMISM	ACTIONS THAT CONVEY DYNAMISM	ACTIONS THAT DERAIL DYNAMISM
Enthusiasm	• Being an enthusiastic learner • Showing your love of the job and the mission you are on for students • Showing a sense of humor • Keeping worries in perspective • Maintaining a focus on the core function of the organization—student and staff learning	• Lacking passion and joy for the people and the work • Isolating from staff and students on a regular basis • Being fake or disingenuous in interactions with team members • Being uptight and anxious on a regular basis
Future Possibilities	• Connecting with your *why* and sharing it with the school community • Being on the lookout for great work and letting people know how much it is appreciated	• Not recognizing and celebrating the achievements of others • Not investing the time and effort to learn what you do not know • Allowing distractions to take the focus from the most important work

(Continued)

(Continued)

FACET OF DYNAMISM	ACTIONS THAT CONVEY DYNAMISM	ACTIONS THAT DERAIL DYNAMISM
Engaging, Interesting, and Credible Resources	• Checking the credibility of all sources before suggesting, using, or securing services for staff	• Relying on hearsay and questionable sources • Failing to source your information in ways that are transparent to others
Confidence	• Seeking and embracing feedback as opportunities to improve • Communicating with confidence based on your expertise	• Being overconfident in the absence of competence • Flip-flopping on important decisions or values to gain political favor

PRACTICES TO STRENGTHEN DYNAMISM

As you have learned in this chapter, your passion and excitement about the work you do with your team have a direct impact on people's engagement with you at work. Low-energy, dispassionate, or inaccurate communication will result in the same from teachers, students, and families and have a significant impact on their assessment of your credibility as an effective leader. Following are suggested strategies that may strengthen your dynamism. At the end of this section, you will be able to rate them based on the level of challenge they present to you, and they may ultimately help you decide how to proceed.

Ramp up enthusiasm and joy at work. Passion, enthusiasm, and excitement are chosen attitudes and are contagious. To build your dynamism, intentionally decide to be enthusiastic at work. This doesn't mean that you never have a bad day or that the work suddenly becomes less stressful, however; it is how you respond to the daily stressors and how you regulate your state of mind that makes a difference to the people who work with you. Teachers, students, and families want to learn with and from dynamic leaders and they will, in turn, become committed followers. Nobody wants to work with a negative, pessimistic leader. We recognize that the past few years have been complex and exhausting for school leaders especially, but students are back in school, with more needs than ever. Dynamic leadership, therefore, is needed now more than ever. Find what gives you joy at work. Tap into your why and help others do the same. Build teams and foster collaboration. Take every opportunity to demonstrate your belief in possibilities and your confidence in staff to make great things happen for learners every day.

Become an engaging speaker. A large part of becoming a dynamic leader is the ability to engage people in the messages you share. Learn how to speak with confidence and enthusiasm when making presentations. Strengthen your presentation skills by avoiding vocal hesitancies such as "umm," "you know," and "okay." Practice speaking clearly with a purposeful tone, while varying the tone, inflection, and volume of your voice. Use gestures, eye contact, and movement around the room to sustain interest. Speak from the heart. Infuse interesting stories. Personal stories and interesting videos or pictures can bring a point to life for listeners and inspire them to act in ways that are consistent with your message. Learn how to create slide presentations that are visually interesting and thought provoking for participants. There are many resources available to help you. The general advice is to limit the amount of text on a slide to seven to 10 words and choose images that convey the point you want to make.

Ensure source credibility. Be careful in selecting sources, print, media, and/or individuals to validate the work you want to do. Sources should be grounded in expertise developed by actually doing the work and experiencing and producing results. Be aware that sources may contain bias or hidden agendas and rely on misinformation or cherry-picked information to persuade or influence your next steps. Use the tools provided in this chapter to make source decisions you can stand by and that provide the validation and support you need to impact the success of your school.

Engage in deliberate practice to improve. Deliberate practice means that you will engage in improving one or two aspects of becoming a dynamic leader, over time with purposeful action toward getting better. Essential to your growth in dynamism will be seeking and acting on feedback from staff on the factors that make a leader dynamic. This feedback, coupled with honest, accurate self-assessment, will position you for real self-improvement in this area of leadership credibility. Use the tools shared in this chapter to develop a limited number of survey questions for staff and then create a plan to deliberately practice in those areas that need improvement. Regularly seek anecdotal feedback as well from trusted colleagues or staff members who can provide evidence of your growth. Track your growth over time and celebrate your success!

PAUSE AND PONDER

► How challenging would it be for you to adopt one or more of the four strategies provided here? Would it be easy because you already do it? Do any of the strategies pose a significant challenge for you? Why? What would it take to overcome it?

CONCLUSION

Teachers are drawn to dynamic leaders who are passionate about the work and the people they lead, and it is these very people who determine a leader's credibility based on the qualities you have learned about so far in this book. Dynamism does not require charismatic leadership, but it does require passion, commitment, and inspiration for staff to engage deeply in the work with you. We have observed leaders across the country who demonstrate dynamism in a soft-spoken, mild-mannered, and calm manner and are also excited and passionate about the success of their schools, their teams, and their learners.

Leaders who struggle with low confidence will have difficulty projecting dynamism as well as effectively conducting meetings, initiating performance discussions, and leading the organization overall. In fact, a leader's lack of self-confidence has more of a negative effect than high self-confidence has a positive effect. In other words, self-confidence seems to pull overall leadership effectiveness down more than it pushes it up (Folkman, 2021).

In the bigger picture, leadership is a service. Leaders exist to serve a purpose for the people who have made it possible for them to lead—their constituents. Credible leaders know that it is through their visible actions that their true commitment is demonstrated. They spend their time—the trust indicator of priorities—on things that matter most to learning. They audit how their time is spent and determine how well the proportions relate to the importance of the shared values. They hold themselves accountable to the same standards as everyone else, and when their leadership is inadequate, they make amends for it, just as they would expect others to do, and these actions help them build their credibility to make a greater impact.

CHAPTER 4

....

IMMEDIACY

Verbal and Nonverbal Indicators of Relatedness

Before we begin our discussion on immediacy, take a few minutes to respond to the self-assessment in Figure 4.1, which reflects the main ideas and elements in activating immediacy behaviors. This information can help you focus on the content that matters most to you as you read through the chapter.

FIGURE 4.1 IMMEDIACY SELF-ASSESSMENT
....

IMMEDIACY					
ITEM #	SURVEY ITEM	3 ALWAYS	2 SOMETIMES	1 RARELY	0 NEVER
1.	My verbal and nonverbal communication signifies a genuine interest in others.				

(Continued)

(Continued)

ITEM #	SURVEY ITEM	3 ALWAYS	2 SOMETIMES	1 RARELY	0 NEVER
IMMEDIACY					
2.	I am intentional about being accessible and visible to staff, students, and parents.				
3.	I enjoy being among staff and students and sitting with them at their tables and in their groups while they are working.				
4.	I strive for partnership relationships with school team members to enable joint effort and commitment to reaching school goals.				
Mean for Immediacy *(Total divided by 4)*					

REAL REFLECTION

Which of the indicators of immediacy are strengths for you?

Which of the indicators present growth opportunities?

What conclusions are you drawing about the immediacy between you and people who work in your school or district?

Whom can you enlist to support you in strengthening your immediacy and thus building your credibility?

People crave connections and interpersonal relationships. After all, we are social animals and the evidence clearly indicates the pervasive need for people to form bonds with other humans (e.g., Hawkley & Cacioppo, 2010). Of course, some of these relationships are personal and others are professional. On the professional level, we want to feel a sense of belonging to the organization and with the people inside the organization, especially our leaders. We want to trust and be trusted, which we discussed in Chapter 1. And we expect effective communication systems to be developed. These interpersonal relationships are always in play inside an organization. The closeness and belonging that some people experience is known as *immediacy*, defined as "the degree of perceived physical or psychological closeness between two people" (Richmond et al., 2012, p. 368).

Immediacy involves the creation and maintenance of interpersonal connections between leaders and group members (Wilson & Locker, 2007–2008). Immediacy is the primary way that humans indicate a personal closeness, a willingness to communicate, and positive feelings about others. The concept of immediacy was introduced by social psychologist Albert Mehrabian, who noted that "people are drawn toward persons and things they like, evaluate highly, and prefer; and they avoid or move away from things they dislike, evaluate negatively, or do not prefer" (1971, p. 1). Immediacy brings people together, but a lack of immediacy creates emotional distances between people. And that's the last thing that leaders want—distance between them and the people they supervise.

Importantly, immediacy is not friendships. Being friendly and open, developing supportive relations, and conveying warmth all contribute to the sense of immediacy. But that does not mean that you must be friends with the people at work. As Foster (2019) noted, there are ways to use immediacy in leadership, including

- Being visibly engaged

- Making frequent small talk

- Leading with questions

- Making appropriate physical contact (handshake, high five, etc.)

- Finding opportunities to laugh with your staff members (Foster, 2019)

PAUSE AND PONDER

▶ Use the bulleted list from Foster to identify some of your immediacy actions. These are general statements and we will explore immediacy in greater detail. For now, consider your actions.

VERBAL AND NONVERBAL IMMEDIACY

The field of immediacy is divided into two parts: verbal and nonverbal. Verbal and nonverbal actions can send positive messages of liking and closeness, decrease the psychological distance between people, and positively affect motivation (e.g., Dalonges & Fried, 2016).

Early indicators of immediacy focused on nonverbal items such as smiles and gestures. Mandal (2014) identified a range of nonverbal items related to immediacy, including

- Kinesics, the study of body movements when communicating

- Gestures and facial expressions

- Proxemics, the nature, degree, and effect of the spatial separation individuals naturally maintain

- Eye movement

- Touching behaviors (e.g., handshake, high five)

As Talley and Temple (2018) noted, even our hand gestures create nonverbal immediacy. They created a list of hand gestures that are positive versus those that indicate defensiveness (see Figure 4.2).

FIGURE 4.2 DIFFERENCES IN HAND GESTURES

HAND GESTURES THAT ARE POSITIVE	HAND GESTURES THAT ARE DEFENSIVE
• Community hands (the position of the hands shows the palm vertical to the ground)	• Hands in pockets (both hands are in the leader's pants pockets)
• Humility hands (hands are clasped in front of the person at waist level)	• Crossed arms (both arms are crossed over the chest)
• Steepling hands (hands form a steeple with fingertips touching)	• Hands behind back (hands are clasped behind the back)

SOURCE: Talley and Temple (2018).

Andrea Lockhart loved being a teacher—she loved the interaction with students and she especially loved Fridays. She didn't love Fridays because they represented the end of the week; she loved Fridays because she had "High-Five Fridays." Every student that entered her class knew that on Friday they were leaving with a big smile and an even bigger high five. Recently, Ms. Lockhart took on the role of vice principal in a neighboring district and helped facilitate the professional development meetings. She noticed that some of her colleagues came in tired and exhausted from the week and didn't have a lot of energy during the meetings. She thought to herself, "I want my colleagues to know that I'm here for them." Then she remembered High-Five Fridays and reestablished the tradition, bringing back the high five to the professional development sessions. Now, Ms. Lockhart stands at the door and welcomes every person with a high five as they enter. That little high five and the eye contact that goes with it helps spark connection and lets people know she sees them.

PAUSE AND PONDER

▶ What do your nonverbal behaviors create immediacy? Can you video record yourself and analyze your nonverbal behaviors, including hand gestures?

In addition to nonverbal indicators, there are verbal indicators such as providing personal examples (self-disclosure), asking questions, using humor, addressing others by name, praising others, initiating discussion, and using inclusive pronouns ("we" versus "I") that also convey immediacy. The goal of verbal immediacy indicators includes making sure that the receivers feel valued, important, and heard. In addition to the words we use, our vocal behavior contributes to immediacy. As McCroskey (2005) noted, there are six vocal qualities that impact your ability to be a persuasive speaker:

- Volume control

- Rate of speech

- Use of pitch

- Articulation

- Fluency with effective pauses

Although the verbal indicators are important, Mehrabian (1972) notes that 93% of interpersonal attitude is communicated nonverbally. If your verbal indicators do not match your nonverbal indicators, the nonverbal ones will dominate, and that's the message that will be received.

We have focused on immediacy from a leader's perspective, but there has been considerable research about immediacy in the classroom. Wilson and Locker (2007–2008) identified actions that fostered immediacy in the classroom. In Figure 4.3, you'll find their original indicators from their work with college students and then the ones that we modified for school leaders. Note that some are negative (e.g., *using a monotone voice*), as their study was to see which factors correlated with higher levels of learning. You might use the teacher column to support a colleague who needs to develop immediacy with students and the leadership column to reflect on your own actions.

FIGURE 4.3 INDICATORS OF IMMEDIACY

CLASSROOM INDICATORS OF IMMEDIACY	POSSIBLE EDUCATIONAL LEADERSHIP INDICATORS OF IMMEDIACY
1. Uses personal examples or talks about personal experiences	1. Uses personal examples or talks about personal experiences
2. Asks questions or encourages students to talk	2. Asks questions or encourages students to talk
3. Gets into discussions based on something a student brings up even when it doesn't seem to be part of the lecture plan	3. Engages in discussions based on something a staff member identifies
4. Uses humor in class	4. Uses humor appropriately
5. Addresses students by name	5. Addresses staff by name
6. Addresses me by name	6. N/A
7. Gets into conversations with individual students before or after class	7. Engages in conversations with individuals on an informal basis
8. Has initiated conversations with me before, after, or during class	8. Initiates individual, informal conversations with staff
9. Refers to class as "our class" and says "what we are doing"	9. Refers to school or district as "ours" and says "what we are doing"
10. Provides feedback on my individual work through comments on papers, oral discussions, etc.	10. Provides feedback on my individual work
11. Calls on students to answer questions even if they have not indicated that they want to talk	11. N/A
12. Asks students how they felt about an assignment	12. Asks staff how they felt about their work
13. Invites students to telephone or meet outside of class if they have a question or want to discuss something	13. Invites staff to text, talk, or meet if they have a question or want to discuss something

(Continued)

(Continued)

CLASSROOM INDICATORS OF IMMEDIACY	POSSIBLE EDUCATIONAL LEADERSHIP INDICATORS OF IMMEDIACY
14. Asks questions to solicit viewpoints or opinions	14. Asks questions to solicit viewpoints or opinions
15. Praises students' work, actions, or comments	15. Praises staff's work, actions, or comments
16. Will have discussions about things unrelated to class with individual students or with the class as a whole	16. Will have discussions about things unrelated to the current focus with individual staff members or with the whole group
17. Has invited students to use their first name (again, remember that this was college level)	17. Has invited staff to use their first name
18. Gestures while talking to the class	18. Gestures while talking
19. Uses a monotone/dull voice while talking to the class	19. N/A
20. Looks at the class while talking	20. Looks at individuals while talking
21. Smiles at the class as a whole, not just a few select students	21. Smiles at various members of the whole group, not just a few select staff
22. Has a tense body position while talking to the class	22. Has a tense body position while talking
23. Moves around the classroom while teaching	23. Moves around the campus or room while teaching

SOURCE: Wilson and Locker (2007–2008).

This reminds us of the research on teacher actions when it comes to students they believe to be low performing (e.g., Good, 1987). The list above has useful considerations for general interactions with staff. Now consider teachers or staff members you believe are low performing. Do any of the unconscious actions teachers display toward students appear in the ways you interact with staff? In other words, are staff members who are perceived to be low achieving

- Criticized more often for failure?
- Praised less frequently?
- Receiving less feedback?
- Being called on less often?
- Having less eye contact from you?
- Having fewer friendly interactions with you?
- Experiencing acceptance of their ideas less often?

If your answer to any of these is *yes*, then you likely need to address the issue and re-recruit the staff member(s), while changing your nonverbal and verbal actions to increase immediacy.

Principal Cynthia Lawson and vice principal Jerimiah Gray noticed that when they engaged in brief conversations with the teachers at their school, they saw an upswing in the morale of the staff. Recently they saw a dip in that morale, so they implemented small wins spotlights. They asked all the grade-level teams to start meetings with small wins from the week. These conversations occurred and teachers seemed pleased to be recognized, but the leaders realized that this change wasn't helping the staff understand how thankful and appreciated the leaders were. These leaders decided to recognize staff members' small wins in writing. The leaders created postcards with the sentence "I saw your small win" already printed on them. Ms. Lawson and Mr. Gray added the small win they observed and sent the postcard to the person's home. This generated a buzz around campus as teachers said, "Leadership sees me." As one teacher noted, "I get spotlighted at school and also at home."

IMMEDIACY THROUGH ACTIVE AND EMPATHETIC LISTENING

Thus far, we have focused on the verbal and nonverbal behaviors of the leader to build immediacy. Most of these have been the outward actions and behaviors that people can use to clearly communicate a sense of closeness, relatedness, and connection. What we have not focused on is how people feel heard and the impact that listening plays on immediacy.

There are two types of listening that are especially powerful in fostering immediacy.

The first is active listening. Rather than paying partial attention, when we actively listen, we give our full attention to the person. We make a conscious effort to hear, understand, and remember the information that is being shared. And this type of listening is more than just attending to the words that are used. Much like the nonverbal communication that is sent, during actively listening, you also notice the nonverbal communication you are receiving. Consider the following list of active listening skills:

- Give the person your full and undivided attention and eliminate environmental distractions. This may include changing the setting for the conversation.

- Avoid thinking about what you're going to say next. The opposite of speaking isn't waiting to speak again. It's listening.

- Remember key words or phrases and repeat them, but don't comment on them. In doing so, you demonstrate that you are attuned to the speaker.

- Ask open-ended questions that invite elaboration or speculation. "When you say that you're crushed by what happened, what do you mean? What did that feel like when it happened, and how is it feeling now?"

- When it is necessary for you to comment, use "I" statements. "What I think I am understanding is . . ." invites the person to acknowledge or clarify the accuracy of the message.

- Don't interrupt.

 PAUSE AND PONDER

▶ Consider your active listening skills and identify areas that you may need to attend to.

Michael P. Nichols, the author of *The Lost Art of Listening*, advises using active listening techniques "to let them be themselves while [you] continue to be [yourself]" (1995, p. 250). In other words, you don't have to make a personal connection with everything that the other person shares. And you don't need to tell stories that show the speaker that you have had worse experiences. This is not the time to one-up the speaker.

Empathetic listening extends to active listening. Empathetic listening is a structured approach to listening and questioning that allows you to develop and maintain relationships. Carl Rogers, who pioneered nondirective therapy, believed that power was often used to shut down conversations. Thomas Gordon, a student of Rogers, developed "I" messages to build empathetic listening and reflective thinking. Gordon (2003) incorporated these into a teacher effectiveness training program as a means for educators to interact constructively with students. But they are not limited to teachers. In fact, the business world has focused intensively on empathetic listening. For example, Schmitz (2016) notes that there are steps to empathetic listening, including:

- Say what you hear. Simply repeat what you hear in order to get further understanding. Repeat it exactly as you think you heard it.

- Reflect on the feeling. Try to understand the feeling expressed in what was said, going beyond what you think you heard.

- Restate what was said and think about the feeling. This combines the previous steps in order to understand the message.

As leaders, we also need to be listened to. How do you know if you are in the presence of someone who is empathetically listening to you? Figure 4.4 lists some signs to look for; can you incorporate these into your practice?

FIGURE 4.4 HOW DO YOU KNOW YOU ARE IN THE PRESENCE OF AN EMPATHIC LISTENER?

They are in the "listening position." The person listening to you is maintaining eye contact with you. Their hands and body are still, and they aren't fidgeting or tapping their foot. They are leaning in and may even tilt their head slightly to improve their hearing.

They resist interrupting you. Interruption interferes with the flow of your processing. An empathic listener allows for pauses. They create space for you to gather your thoughts and notice the insights you are reaching.

Their interjections are encouraging. They may smile or nod when appropriate and use words of encouragement when the topic is a difficult one (for example, "Take your time").

They paraphrase what you're saying. They might restate an idea or label an emotion (for example, "You'd like to change the way you are facilitating the group but feeling frustrated about the strategies you've tried").

They ask open-ended questions to clarify their own understanding. Empathetic listeners pose questions that are speculative and nonjudgmental. For instance, they might ask, "Why do you think that is the case?" or "Given your knowledge of this department, where do you think their strengths lie?"

They help you move toward your goal. Rather than launching into a description of what they would have done, they stay focused on what you hope to achieve. They might say something like, "You're looking to find a new way to help this group be more productive and reduce the conflicts they seem to have." Stating your goal provides a way of organizing your thoughts so that you can move to solutions.

They don't give advice unless you ask for it. Empathetic listeners understand that many times the answer lies within, and their role is to assist you in locating it. If invited to provide advice, they will.

As a leader, you will experience the growing pains of having a "family" away from your family at home. Schools create an environment where individuals must work hand in hand with one another, and sometimes this takes place for years. Sometimes that close contact and multiple encounters can result in frustrations. These frustrations are often brought to the attention of a leader who is tasked with mending the situation.

Recently, the seventh-grade team had their monthly meeting. Their focus during this session was the common challenge of academic vocabulary. They had agreed that every teacher would have a vocabulary wall in their room and that the vocabulary wall would be used to teach, practice, and reinforce academic word learning. During the meeting, Sarah Hayley asked everyone to share photos of their walls and to spotlight some of the successes they had had. Joseph Branch explained that his history class did not have a vocabulary wall because they were creating an online resource for vocabulary and that he didn't want that on his walls, adding that he felt it was very elementary.

Ms. Hayley was visibly upset and said that this was a team decision. She added, "We should all be doing what we agreed to so that students would have consistency across the school day." She felt defeated at the end of the meeting and went to her leader to discuss these feelings. She explained to the principal, Kendra Prince, that no matter what she did in the team meeting, she had one or two teachers that would push back on the conversation even though they created the challenge together. She said she felt that she shouldn't be leading the team anymore. As Ms. Prince heard the frustration, and maybe even the hurt, in Ms. Hayley's voice, she addressed her by saying

> I can hear that you are frustrated and I know that frustration comes from how much effort you have put into this team. I hear your commitment to making sure the grade-level PLC runs strong so it benefits our students. I hope you recognize where you have taken this team and are able to celebrate that. I also hear that at least one colleague wants to have the same common challenge but would be interested in showcasing it in a different way. Is that a fair estimate?

In this moment, the leader heard Ms. Hayley's feelings, displayed empathy for those feelings, and started to also show empathy to the other colleague as well. This form of empathic listening allowed the leader to help Ms. Hayley to start reframing her thinking about the situation and how she could respond to similar situations in the future.

IMMEDIACY THROUGH BEING THERE

Where you put your body communicates a lot to the people who work with you. We have lost count of the number of times we have been invited to provide professional learning opportunities and the leaders are nowhere to be found. Sure, there are pressing priorities and crises that leaders must attend to, but when they fail to make their presence known in a given environment, such as professional learning, it signals to others that this is not very important.

Of course, leaders cannot be everywhere, and everyone on the staff knows that. But developing a pattern of missing certain gatherings, such as professional learning sessions, grade-level or department meetings, IEP meetings, and such, sends a message to the members that there is always something more important happening at that time. We encourage you to review the gatherings that are planned for each week and to strategically attend some of them.

Of course, it's more than being physically present. Sitting in the back of the room to respond to emails might even be worse for your credibility than not attending at all. As many leadership experts have noted, you should model the way. That means that you are an active participant in the session and are engaging with the content as you would expect others to do. Keep in mind there is a balance to be struck between participating too much and inviting others to engage with you. You'll recall from Chapter 2, on competence, that coordination of attentiveness is a signal of your communication competence.

Remember, you're always on display and people are watching your moves to identify what you value. When staff members feel connected with you, and they see how you engage with others, your credibility grows, as does your impact on others.

► Did you attend the most recent professional development session with teachers? For how long? Did you engage with the content? How might you attend parts of professional learning sessions so that you are knowledgeable?

THE FALLACY OF AN OPEN-DOOR POLICY

It is common in leadership to boast of an "open-door policy" in which staff members are encouraged to stop by an office to meet informally, ask a few questions, or talk about something that is on their minds. There are several reasons why this may not be the best idea, including the fact that school leaders should not spend considerable amounts of time in the office. Instead, they should spend time in places where learning is occurring. After all, that's our business: learning. And we're not going to be able to influence learning, much less maximize effective practices, from an office removed from classrooms.

In addition, as Kruse (2016a) noted, some employees are afraid to speak up, and the open-door policy requires that they find you in your office and initiate the conversation. Teachers rarely have time to do this as they spend the vast majority of their workday with students. But even if they did find the time and found you in the office, the courage required to start the conversation may be more than some people could muster.

Kruse (2016b) notes that an open-door policy has the potential to create employees who are overly dependent on leaders. Some will check in with you for every decision and ask for validation for each action and thus take no responsibility for the outcomes. True, there are some decisions that rest with leaders, but teachers make thousands of decisions each day and must learn to trust their decisional capabilities. Further, open-door policies can turn leaders into therapists and prevent them from accomplishing other responsibilities that are equally important.

Andrew Foster believed that he was doing the right thing by leaving his office door open and inviting people to come in and talk with him as needed. Emerson Jones stopped by several times per week to get advice and let Mr. Foster know what was happening in the front office. The time commitment was averaging more than three hours per week—time away from classrooms and learning. Of course, the front office is an important part of the school and the staff there deserve time and attention, but only Mr. Jones was using the office hours. There must be a more effective and efficient way to ensure that people feel free to share important information with the leader. And leaders need to think about equitable distribution of their time so that they maintain immediacy with everyone who works at the school or district.

IMMEDIACY THROUGH ROUNDING

Perhaps, as Kruse (2016b) notes, leaders need to hold regular one-on-one meetings. These do not have to be formal sit-down sessions; instead, they can be rounding conversations that provide each person an opportunity to share with you, rather than relying on the courage of a few who are willing to initiate. During rounding times, visit teachers and staff members, but not with a focus on instruction—when you make rounds, you are looking to recognize what is working and improve things that are not. You can ask questions such as

- What is working well today?
- Are there individuals I should be recognizing? (Then acknowledge the people that are named.)
- Is there anything we can do better? (Take notes and work to address the recommendations.)
- Do you have the tools and equipment you need to do your job? (If they need something, work to obtain it.)

In addition, Kruse (2016b) recommends keeping a schedule of group meetings. In his words, this builds a "rhythm of communication" that touches all employees and ensures that there are regular opportunities to develop immediacy. Spending time in the company of groups allows you to provide and receive information in a much more systematic way. As we noted in the previous section, it's important to review the various gatherings each week and make conscious decisions about which ones you will attend so that you can maximize your return on investment.

We are suggesting not that you ban staff members from coming to you to share something, but rather that you take a more proactive approach and develop systems to engage with each person who reports to you on a regular basis. Not only does this facilitate immediacy, but it also increases the likelihood that you remain informed about the needs and strengths of your teams.

LEADERSHIP PRACTICES THAT CONVEY AND DERAIL IMMEDIACY

Facial expressions, tone of voice, and body language can all betray the emotions of a leader. And staff can be highly attuned to the nonverbal signals a leader makes. Couple these with habitually late arrivals and dominating some discussions while being a nonparticipant in others, and you'll soon have a reputation that you are not responsive to others. Examine Figure 4.5 on actions that convey and derail immediacy. Have you been on the receiving end of any of these?

FIGURE 4.5 CONVEYING AND DERAILING OUR IMMEDIACY

FACET OF IMMEDIACY	ACTIONS THAT CONVEY IMMEDIACY	ACTIONS THAT DERAIL IMMEDIACY
Nonverbal	• Smiling • Using open facial expressions • Making eye contact • Using non-threatening gestures • Displaying relaxed body language	• Frowning • Looking bored or demonstrating disinterest • Looking annoyed • Failing to make eye contact • Staring • Making closed fists

(Continued)

(Continued)

FACET OF IMMEDIACY	ACTIONS THAT CONVEY IMMEDIACY	ACTIONS THAT DERAIL IMMEDIACY
Nonverbal (continued)	• Positioning at an appropriate distance • Arriving early for appointments	• Keeping hands behind back • Displaying tense or on-guard body language • Arriving late; the meeting doesn't really start until you get there
Verbal	• Using gentle humor • Using a friendly tone • Responding in a timely way • Asking questions and opinions of others	• Using humor that humiliates • Shaming others • Using a harsh tone • Delaying response in the hope that it will be forgotten • Dominating the discussion • Interrupting others

PAUSE AND PONDER

▶ Actions that derail immediacy are easy to recognize in others but more difficult to see in our own behaviors. With permission from others, video record yourself in a short meeting and analyze your own actions. What do you want to strengthen?

PRACTICES TO STRENGTHEN IMMEDIACY

Following are suggested strategies that may strengthen your ability to activate immediacy behaviors that foster a greater connectedness to your staff. At the end of this section, think about the Pause and Ponder questions that can help you decide how to proceed.

Use rounding to increase your immediacy. Walkthroughs to observe classroom instruction are common, but finding out what people need is less so. Put weekly rounding walks in your schedule to learn about what people need. In the process, you can learn a tremendous amount about them, their context, and their challenges. If you are a site administrator, the regular practice of rounding can also serve to lower the affective filter that many teachers feel when the principal walks into the classroom. You can see them (and often their students) tense up as soon as you cross the threshold. Build a habit and an expectation on their part that your presence in their room isn't strictly evaluative. It further builds your credibility as a leader who genuinely cares for their well-being.

When something needs to be done, don't pass it on to others. Be self-aware about the hierarchy present in any organization and do what you can to help flatten it a bit. If the cafeteria tables need to be moved quickly to set up for a professional development session, and you're physically capable of doing so, pitch in. If you see a frazzled teacher at the copier, step in to see if you can assist. People appreciate when leaders are willing to roll up their sleeves to help make the day run a bit smoother for someone else. One of our very favorite memories was doing a learning walk with John Hattie. We were in a 10th-grade integrated math classroom. Guess who passed out the handouts for the teacher? Her eyes got as big as saucers. But that's just the kind of leader John is.

CONCLUSION

This chapter has focused on verbal and nonverbal behaviors that tell people that they are important, valued, and connected with you as a leader. Taken together, these factors of immediacy create a climate in which people are best able to do their work. When staff members do not feel connected with the leader (or with each other, for that matter) their confidence can be negatively impacted and they question whether this is the right place for them to work, or not.

Leaders are always being watched. Where we put our bodies, how we interact with others, and what we pay attention to sends strong messages through the school or district and lets people know what we believe is important. Leaders need to use their immediacy skills to connect with each staff member so that the entire team is working in concert to improve the learning lives of students and make the workplace rewarding. Immediacy helps people to realize that their school is the best place for them to learn, the best place for them to work, and the best place for them to teach.

CHAPTER 5

....

FORWARD THINKING TO BE FUTURE READY

Welcome to the last chapter on building leader credibility! You have probably learned much about the qualities of credible leaders and are ready to get to work. But don't go too soon. This chapter focuses on the characteristic that distinguishes leader from teacher credibility—that is, being a forward thinker! As you have done in previous chapters, respond to the items in the self-assessment in Figure 5.1 and consider the REAL Reflection questions to get a good sense of your skills and abilities in being a forward-thinking leader.

FIGURE 5.1 FORWARD-THINKING SELF-ASSESSMENT

FORWARD THINKING					
ITEM #	SURVEY ITEM	3 ALWAYS	2 SOMETIMES	1 RARELY	0 NEVER
1.	I routinely allot time for reading professional journals, listening to podcasts, attending webinars, going to conferences, and/or engaging in book studies to learn about trends and best practices in education.				
2.	I have communicated and collaborated with staff on a vision for the future that is both aspirational and inspirational for staff and students.				
3.	I engage the leadership team in conversations by asking questions like *What's new? What's next? What's better for our staff and students?*				
4.	I routinely collect and share evidence with staff on our progress toward our future state and collaborate on the next best steps.				

FORWARD THINKING					
ITEM #	SURVEY ITEM	3 ALWAYS	2 SOMETIMES	1 RARELY	0 NEVER
5.	I intentionally demonstrate a sense of optimism and hope for a better future for our school, especially during tough times.				
6.	I show care and concern for the people I work with and try to demonstrate empathy in interactions.				
Mean for Forward Thinking *(Total divided by 6)*					

REAL REFLECTION

Which of the indicators of forward thinking are strengths for you?

Which of the indicators present growth opportunities?

What conclusions are you drawing about your ability to be forward thinking?

Whom can you enlist to support you in strengthening your work as a forward thinker and thus building your credibility?

FORWARD-THINKING LEADERSHIP

Let's begin with a discussion about Tia Neale. Ms. Neale was in the fourth year of her principalship at a middle school in southeastern Virginia. Her school performed on par with the state average and the parents were generally satisfied with the teachers and the school overall. Ms. Neale was invited to attend a "visioning the future" session hosted by the local Chamber of Commerce with the goal of developing a clear and inspiring vision for the city. As a member of the school system, Ms. Neale served an important role in the work.

Ms. Neale learned a great deal about the importance of "forward thinking" and being "future ready" during these sessions and she came to the realization that, like the work the Chamber of Commerce was doing on behalf of the city, she should be doing similar work on behalf of her school. She began to self-question: *Do my teachers and staff have a clear vision of where we a going as a school? Do they know how they fit into the vision? Do I communicate in ways that help them engage in the vision? Am I thinking forward far enough in the future? Am I, and is my school, future ready?* These questions nagged at Ms. Neale both during and after the workshops and she became inspired to invest her time and energy in developing her skills to forward thinking and vision about the future of her school.

She began by setting aside time each week to read professional journals, listen to podcasts on current educational topics, participate in webinars by respected educational thought leaders, and sign up for book studies when time allowed. She also developed a keen interest in the speeches, presentations, and conversations conducted with various groups by her central office leaders. She read the books they talked about and attended community meetings where the schools were in focus. She rejoined her state's administrator organization to become better informed about state developments related to education.

Ms. Neale recognized that focusing all of her time on putting out fires around the school and not protecting time for her own learning was doing harm to the future of her school.

She decided to invite members of the leadership team to read educational articles and research and share their new learning at team meetings. She added a standing agenda item for members to share and teach the team about important topics they were reading about. She, too, shared her new learning with the team and enjoyed doing so. This led naturally to conversations about the future direction of the school and necessary steps to prepare the staff and students for what they could see was coming down the pike. Of course, this was not where Ms. Neale's work ended; rather, it represented where her work in becoming a forward-thinking leader began.

PAUSE AND PONDER

▶ How well do you currently protect time for your own learning each week? How prepared are you to have forward-thinking conversations with the people on your team(s)?

According to Kouzes and Posner (2009), based on their extensive research into leadership generally, and credibility specifically, leaders must be able to answer the question "Where are we going?" Kouzes and Posner based this conclusion on data from survey responses from tens of thousands of working people around the world. The survey asked respondents "What do you look for and admire in a leader (defined as someone whose direction you would willingly follow)?" and "What do you look for and admire in a colleague (defined as someone you'd like to have on your team)?" *Honesty* was the number-one requirement of a leader, and it was the top response for attributes of a good colleague. There was no difference in the top attributes for what people look for in leaders and in colleagues.

The second-most admired attribute of a leader, however, with 72% of respondents in agreement, turned out to be that they are forward looking, while only 27% of respondents selected it as something they want in a colleague. Interestingly, for respondents holding more senior roles in organizations, the percentage was even greater, with 88% in agreement. No other attribute showed such a dramatic difference between leader and colleague. Being forward-looking, envisioning exciting possibilities, and enlisting others in a shared view of the future is the attribute that most distinguishes leaders from non-leaders. It is important that school leaders recognize the power of this credibility trait and understand that it is what people want most from leaders, outside of honesty.

Philip Tetlock, a professor at the University of Pennsylvania, conducts studies on why some leaders are better at predicting future trends than others. He has identified the common traits in people who have demonstrated in his studies the ability to accurately forecast future trends. These traits are

1. Pragmatic

2. Curious

3. Cautious

4. Humble

5. Open-minded to diverse points of view

6. Alert to personal bias and wishful thinking

7. Think in terms of probabilities to avoid guessing

8. Comfortable with numbers, but not feeling that they need to be mathematicians

Tetlock believes that leaders can get better at forward thinking by monitoring their own skills, knowledge, habits, and practices related to forward thinking (Tucker, 2020).

In school leadership, from the superintendent to teacher-leaders, the list of traits reported by Tetlock is exceedingly relevant. To be a forward-thinking leader in schools, we have to open our minds to doing things differently and better. We have to recognize that we all have biases that we bring to the job and that an awareness of these biases can help in opening us to new research and ideas. We have to discipline ourselves to not be so engrossed in the challenges of the day that we forget that staying on top of trends, challenges, and current topics in education is essential to our development and growth as leaders, which is to say, leaders who can effectively plan for the future.

Robert Tucker, the world-renowned consultant with Fortune 500 companies on "systematic innovation" and former professor at the University of California, Los Angeles (UCLA), has conducted studies since the 1980s on the patterns and habits of visionary leaders. He suggests that a leader's ability and willingness to think forward will be a key component of their organizational and personal success, as he posits that the future is coming faster than ever, and it will be more volatile, uncertain, and ambiguous.

The good news is that much like Tetlock, Tucker (2020) believes that being forward thinking is a learned behavior rather than an innate human ability. We can get better at sizing up what is to come, and seizing the inherent opportunities therein, by being curious, outwardly focused on change in all its dimensions, and proactive in our information intake.

WHY FORWARD-THINKING LEADERSHIP MATTERS

Let's revisit the research from Kouzes and Posner. Recall that their research clearly shows that what people want most from their leaders, as opposed to colleagues, is to be forward looking. They want to be part of an organization that is mission driven, goal oriented, and well prepared for the challenges ahead. They depend on and expect their leaders to focus on and guide this work. Workers are inspired by leaders who can envision a future, figure out where the organization must go to succeed, evaluate ideas for pragmatism, and determine if they fit the organization's core mission. Importantly, people want leaders who focus on how people, money, resources, and organizational capabilities will work together to move from the present to a desired future.

Without a shared mission, vision for the future, and clear path to get there, people will function at work and comply with the requirements for the job, but they will feel directionless. They will wonder (and maybe say aloud), *Where are we trying to go? What are we trying to accomplish? What's our collective purpose? Why are we doing the work we are doing?* Not having answers to these questions can cause apathy, frustration, and anxiety. For workers in nonprofit organizations like schools, it is even more critical to have a clear understanding of questions like those here. Educators in particular yearn for workplaces where they feel they are making a difference in the lives of children and are accomplishing something important with others that they could not have accomplished alone.

In the volatile teacher recruitment market we find ourselves in, leaders must compete for talented staff. One way to rise above competing schools or districts is to share a compelling vision that candidates can connect to the right way, one that they find exciting and uplifting. It is a teachers' market, and they will choose to work where they feel they can work with others toward something fantastic!

PAUSE AND PONDER

▶ Think of a time when you were fully engaged in your work. You were energized and completely committed to the work. What prompted these feelings? What led to your total engagement? What role did the leader play in your dedication to the goals?

DEVELOPING YOUR SKILLS AS A FORWARD THINKER

As you have learned in the previous chapters of this book, a leader's credibility is determined by followers, and followers look for and expect certain characteristics to deem a leader as credible and worthy of their followers. These qualities include trustworthiness, competence, immediacy, dynamism, and being forward thinking. While the first four qualities are also highly valued in colleagues, it is the quality of being forward thinking that set the leader qualities apart from what people want in colleagues.

This presents a conundrum for aspiring leaders: The trait that most separates leaders from individual contributors is something that they haven't had to demonstrate in prior positions. While the ability to focus on the future separates leaders from teachers and staff, many of us fail to understand and appreciate its importance. Leaders devote almost no time to developing this vital quality, which then becomes a huge barrier to future success. Researchers estimate that only 3% of the typical leader's time is spent envisioning the future (Kouzes & Posner, 2009).

Educational researchers at Stanford University conducted studies on how principals spend their time in schools (Grissom et al., 2013). They followed 100 school leaders in an urban setting for three years and conducted both onsite observations and data collection, including principal survey data and student achievement data. The emphasis was on how much time principals spend engaged in instruction-related work, such as visiting classrooms, attending professional development with staff, coaching teachers, and talking informally with staff about teaching and learning. The rounded results of the research are shown in Figure 5.2.

FIGURE 5.2 PRINCIPAL ACTIVITY DISTRIBUTIONS BY TIME

PRINCIPAL ACTIVITY	PERCENT OF TIME
Administrative duties Email, phone calls, student discipline, cafeteria, car line, etc.	28%
Organizational management Staff supervision, evaluation, performance meetings	21%
Other Central office meetings and workshops, lunch	18%

(Continued)

(Continued)

PRINCIPAL ACTIVITY	PERCENT OF TIME
Internal relations Meetings with parent and student groups, attendance at special events, informal time with students and teachers	15%
Instructional program Curriculum planning, assessment/testing management, resource selection	7%
Daily instruction Classroom walkthroughs, coaching, feedback, PLC meetings	6%
External relations Civic league, Rotary, city events	4%

The message in this study, and in many others like it, is to stress the importance of principals spending more time on instructional leadership. We can see in the results of this study that the principal participants spent on average 13% of their day engaged in instructional leadership. (We are sure it recently dropped to less than that, given that principals' time was consumed with COVID-19–related issues.) The researchers argue that leaders need to spend more than 13% of their time on instruction in order to improve student learning outcomes. We agree.

What is not so strongly emphasized in current research, however, is the importance of principals investing time in their own learning. Principals and other school leaders need to spend time individually and collectively learning about current trends and research in the field. This is critical if one is to be forward thinking and future ready. You'll need to become intensely curious about trends, both inside and outside of your school, district, or state, and you will need to engage everyone in the organization in learning about new ideas in the service of creating a better future. Therefore, leaders should try to set aside dedicated time each week for reading journals, listening to podcasts, attending webinars, etc. so they can lead change efforts confidently in alignment with what will be required of schools in the future. We suggest starting with one hour a week, more if possible, and hope that more time can be allotted as time goes on.

PAUSE AND PONDER

▶ How does the Stanford research on how principals spend their time compare to how you spend your time? How might you carve out time in your week to develop your knowledge and skill as a forward-thinking leader?

Sample Time Analysis

The tool below is based on the research from Grissom and colleagues. We recommend using this or something similar to record how you think you spend your time and then to track how you *actually* spend your time. Then, with intention, make small changes to start to gain more and more time on the things that matter most to student and staff learning. Reflect on your last two weeks at work. Complete Figure 5.3 with your best guess on how you spent your time with percentages in each section. Then record how you actually spend your time for the following two weeks and analyze the results! How accurate were you?

FIGURE 5.3 HOW I SPEND MY TIME

ACTIVITY	HOW I THINK I SPEND MY TIME	HOW I ACTUALLY SPEND MY TIME
Administrative duties Email, phone calls, student discipline, cafeteria, car line, etc.		
Organizational management Staff supervision, evaluation, performance meetings		

(Continued)

ACTIVITY	HOW I THINK I SPEND MY TIME	HOW I ACTUALLY SPEND MY TIME
Other Central office meetings and workshops, lunch		
Internal relations Meetings with parent and student groups, attendance at special events, informal time with students and teachers		
Instructional program Curriculum planning, assessment/ testing management, resource selection		
Daily instruction Classroom walkthroughs, coaching, feedback, PLC meetings		
External Relations Civic league, Rotary, city events		

HOW TO GROW YOUR FUTURE FOCUS

There are three ways to expand your ability to become more future-oriented and hone your leadership effectiveness. In *The Truth About Leadership*, Kouzes and Posner (2010) urge readers to spend time learning about the future through

- Insight
- Outsight
- Foresight

Insight: Explore Your Past

With insight, it is suggested that you learn from and stay connected to your past experiences. What did you experience and learn as a new teacher? As a veteran teacher? In other leadership positions? Do any themes occur? When you know more about yourself and keep your lessons learned in mind, you can see farther ahead and imagine future possibilities.

Outsight: Imagine the Possibilities

To be a credible leader, you need to spend more time reading, thinking, and talking about long-term possibilities. Develop the discipline to spend more time studying the future. Bring others into your learning and engage in their learning, as mentioned in Tia's scenario. Make future thinking a standing agenda item at leadership team meetings, or maybe establish a group for the sole purpose of learning and planning the future.

Foresight: Maintain an Optimistic Outlook

Leaders who learn to be optimistic about life and work are far more likely to be successful than those who view things through a pessimist's lens. Being optimistic doesn't mean ignoring reality or the hardships required to get great results. But optimistic leaders give people the hope, energy, and strength needed to carry on. Additionally, when leaders ask *What's new? What's next? What's better?* through an optimist's lens, a whole new set of exciting possibilities emerge that can connect to constituents' visions and aspirations for the future.

WHY OPTIMISM MATTERS TO FORWARD THINKING

In addition to what you have just read related to foresight, many other researchers have weighed in on the value of optimism, specifically for visioning and forward thinking. According to Warren Bennis, global leadership guru, "Optimists have a sixth sense for possibilities that realists can't or won't see." When it comes to becoming future ready to create a shared vision with staff, leaders must have an optimistic outlook about the future. If you cannot create excitement and engagement in what's to come, your general outlook is that it will not work out.

Psychologist Martin Seligman at the University of Pennsylvania has validated through his research that the most successful leaders are inspired by a sense of optimism. In his best-selling book *Learned Optimism,* he writes that optimists are more successful than equally talented pessimists in business, education, sports, and politics. In one of his studies with Metropolitan Life Insurance Company, he developed the Seligman Attribution Style Questionnaire to sort the pessimists from the optimists during hiring. He followed the performance of both groups over several years. The optimists outsold the pessimists by 20% in year one and by 50% in year two. He concluded that optimism is a critical factor in keeping people engaged in their work, even in the face of poor results or bad news, and that optimists outperform pessimists in the workplace (Seligman, 2006). It is all in the way you see things that drives you to seize opportunities or miss them altogether (Lassiter, 2017).

Credible leaders keep hope alive. Sustaining hope means that leaders are personally there for the team in times of need, as you learned in Chapter 4 on immediacy. An upbeat attitude is always essential, and it's even more important in troubling times. Optimists are proactive and behave in ways that promote well-being. People with high hope have higher aspirations and higher levels of performance.

> According to University of Miami psychologist Charles S. Carver, who has written extensively about optimism, when compared with pessimists, optimists may indeed be
>
> 1. More resilient
>
> 2. Less likely to quit
>
> 3. More likely to work out
>
> 4. Quicker to forgive
>
> 5. Less obsessive
>
> 6. Less stressed
>
> 7. Sounder sleepers
>
> 8. More grateful
>
> 9. More altruistic (Kuster, 2016)

All of these traits contribute to leader well-being and effectiveness as well as help position leaders for success in being forward thinking and visionaries for the future. In fact, it is near impossible for a leader with a pessimistic mindset to be successful in preparing teams for an exciting future.

PAUSE AND PONDER

▶ Would you characterize your outlook on the future as optimistic? Are you able to find opportunities in your difficulties? Do teachers generally respond positively to your new ideas? Do you respond positively to others' new ideas?

Let's learn a bit about Eddie Gomez. Mr. Gomez had been an instructional coach in a city school for seven years. While he was generally upbeat and happy, the onset of the pandemic challenged even Mr. Gomez's outlook on things. Luckily, Mr. Gomez worked in a school that was change-ready. The leadership team routinely talked about their future hopes and dreams for the learners they served. They stayed abreast of current research and made wise choices about the new work they brought into the school. Their principal understood the process of change and gave people time to learn and grapple with new practices and programs without fear of making mistakes or being perfect at something right away.

This kind of culture and routine set of practices served them well when COVID-19 forced the closure of schools. The team quickly jumped into action, learning about the platform the district was going to use for virtual learning and beginning to formulate plans to support teachers in totally transforming the way they did their jobs. Mr. Gomez was going to be the primary trainer of teachers on the new ways to deliver instruction.

Teachers (and Mr. Gomez too) were skeptical at best and petrified at worst about delivering instruction to K–5 students on computers. As the staff struggled to learn to use the new technology, Mr. Gomez intentionally made himself believe that it was going to work out. He developed a sense of humor when he made mistakes teaching the teachers, and he bounced back quickly when things did not go as planned. He became a model of optimism for teachers, and they began to relax and collaborate as a team to slowly get better at their new work. Mr. Gomez's deliberate efforts to activate optimistic thinking were contagious and gave permission for others to do the same. The work was still difficult and stressful, but the example set by Mr. Gomez took the edge off and enabled people to largely stay engaged in this difficult work. As their school reopened, they were able to have discussions grounded in the successes they had had and the challenges they faced now, all grounded in a stronger belief in themselves and what they were able to do under extraordinary circumstances.

PAUSE AND PONDER

▶ When your school closed or had to change as a result of the pandemic, how well was it handled by you and other school leaders? What are lessons learned from those experiences that can be leveraged for the future?

FORWARD-THINKING LEADERS AND THE ROLE OF EMPATHY

In Chapter 4, you learned a great deal about the importance of empathetic listening. This information has prepared you well for the discussion in this section on empathetic leadership. Empathetic leadership is about demonstrating a genuine atmosphere of understanding and a shared vision of meaningfulness that permeates the everyday running of the organization, carrying through from teachers to students to families. Daniel Goleman (2006), psychologist, author of 10 books, and two-time Pulitzer Prize nominee for his work on emotional intelligence, tells us that there are three kinds of empathy that leaders need to develop (see Figure 5.4).

FIGURE 5.4   TYPES OF EMPATHY FOR LEADERS

COGNITIVE EMPATHY	EMOTIONAL EMPATHY	EMPATHETIC CONCERN
Seeing the world through the eyes of staff and students	Connecting to the feelings of staff and students	Expressing care and concern for staff and students

Cognitive empathy is the ability to see the world through another person's eyes. It helps us connect with another person's perspective, giving us a mental sense of how they think and see things. This is a critical skill for leaders wanting to be more forward looking, as it enables strong relationships with staff and students and fosters communication with them to encourage, challenge, and motivate.

Emotional empathy helps leaders to tune in to the feelings of another person and read their facial, vocal, and a stream of other nonverbal signs, which illustrate how they feel. According to Daniel Siegel, a UCLA psychiatrist, connecting with people on this level creates a "we" chemistry in the brain that builds rapport and understanding that results in productive and meaningful work for both parties. Leaders with emotional empathy can become trusted partners with all invested, thereby encouraging risk taking and out-of-the-box thinking to meet challenging goals.

The third type of empathy is empathic concern, or expressing care and concern about another person. You may recall the importance of care and concern for others in your reading in Chapter 1 on relational trust. Leaders accomplish this kind of connection when they show people that they will be supported and that they are cared for. This encourages staff to embrace challenges and open up for collaboration and team learning, just like Mr. Gomez's school had in the scenario presented earlier. Goleman stresses that it is essential for leaders, especially forward-thinking leaders, to have all three kinds of empathy to truly engage staff in forward-focused projects.

McKinsey and Company also conducted research on the essential qualities leaders need to "speak to deeper human needs and engage with the world outside corporate walls"

(Balchandani et al., n.d.). They identified leader traits that underpin their "conscious drive to recognize and understand another person's emotional state":

- Leading by example
- Taking a broad, long-term view of the future
- The ability to connect with and inspire others and create networks
- The ability to tolerate failure

They go on to suggest that the best way to develop empathy is "learning by doing," resulting in a boost in the energy you will inevitably need to succeed in your mission. Roll up your sleeves alongside your teams to experiment and devise the change you want to see and make note of your lessons learned along the way. Exchange ideas with your peers or networks outside of your school and provide the same opportunities for staff. Engaging in forward-focused work is about building relationships, beginning from a place with alignment and shared values.

Forward-focused work cannot incubate in isolated spaces. It comes to life when new ideas and information are brought into the space by forward-thinking, committed individuals. It stays alive and develops legs through nurturing over time by individuals invested in its success.

LEADERSHIP PRACTICES THAT CONVEY AND DERAIL FORWARD THINKING

On the next page, Figure 5.5 provides a list of leader behaviors that can build or detail your efforts to become forward thinking.

We have shared a great deal of information about leader credibility in the previous pages. We have offered opportunities for self-assessment, self-reflection, and the next steps. We have attempted to convey a clear rationale as to why leader credibility deserves the attention and focus of all leaders, but most especially school leaders. We thought it would be interesting for readers to end the book with a list of characteristics that

FIGURE 5.5 CONVEYING AND DERAILING OUR FORWARD THINKING

FACET OF FORWARD THINKING	ACTIONS THAT CONVEY FORWARD THINKING	ACTIONS THAT DERAIL FORWARD THINKING
Time for My Own Learning	• Dedicating time to research and learning about current trends and practices in the field • Encouraging professional reading and sharing at the team meeting • Being a teacher to teachers on new trends and research relevant to your people	• Running around putting out fires all day • Displaying disengagement in professional reading or opportunities
Vision for the Future	• Being a calculated risk taker and challenging the status quo	• Lacking focus on instructional matters • Being afraid to take a risk • Appearing satisfied with the status quo
Continuous Improvement	• Mining new ideas from staff • Supporting the learning process as staff grapple with change	• Being unaccepting of others' ideas for the future • Appearing reluctant to collaborate
Evidence of Impact	• Using qualitative and quantitative data to gauge one's own impact	• Blaming, complaining, and deflecting responsibility • Failing to seek feedback regularly • Relying on stale data • Cherry-picking the data so you look good
Optimism	• Demonstrating optimism about future possibilities and opportunities	• Being isolated from staff • Being unable to connect with staff
Empathy	• Demonstrating empathetic leadership by showing care and concern for people	• Viewing staff members narrowly through job roles rather than appreciating their personal concerns and victories

indicate you are *not* a credible leader. We hope you can learn just a bit more about leader credibility from this list before you go.

FIVE DEAD GIVEAWAYS YOU'RE NOT A CREDIBLE LEADER

1. **You don't live in the real world.** You cannot lead without being engaged and aware. Isolation is one of the great enemies of leadership, assailing credibility at every turn. Sequestered leaders develop a narrow worldview and begin to limit options. Leaders who start to believe their own smoke, and who are more concerned about being right than achieving the right outcome, place their credibility at risk. Passion without perspective or reason can actually serve to distort one's perception of reality.

2. **You don't listen.** The fastest way to erode credibility is to live in a bubble—to fail to listen to those who can make you better. Being a leader does not make you omniscient, but it should give you the wisdom to seek sound advice and counsel. Credible leaders don't selectively listen—their listening switch is always flipped on. They listen not just to a small inner circle, but they listen to those that confront, challenge, stretch, and develop them.

3. **You treat people poorly.** If you want to watch your credibility go up in smoke, it's not that hard to do—just be a jerk. A leader's first obligation is to those they lead. As a leader, you are nothing more, or less, than what you model. If you don't build into and support those you lead, what makes you think they'll behave any differently toward others or toward you?

4. **You're not accountable.** Almost nothing impugns the credibility of a leader faster than attempting to dodge an issue rather than deal with it. [It's been said], "Leaders not accountable to their people will be held accountable by their people." We have too many people in leadership positions who can't or won't accept responsibility for anything. Put simply, leadership is about accountability, not blame-shifting. Leadership *is* ownership. Accepting responsibility for your actions, or

the actions of your team, makes you honorable and trustworthy—it also humanizes you.

5. **You don't perform.** Nothing smacks of poor credibility like a lack of performance. Nobody's perfect, but leaders who consistently fail are not leaders, no matter how much you wish they were. . . . Real leaders perform, they get the job done, and they consistently exceed expectations. *No results equals no leadership*—it's just that simple.

SOURCE: Myatt (2015). From Forbes. © 2015 Forbes. All rights reserved. Used under license.

As you think about these five indicators that you are *not* a credible leader, ask yourself the questions below. This is the ultimate REAL Reflection. If you respond "yes" to any of these questions, the next step is to seek feedback and mentorship from trusted and candid colleagues or coaches to develop a plan to address the issue. As a deputy superintendent once told Cathy when she was a principal, "You have to face it, erase it!"

Do any of these descriptors ring true to you?

- Am I disconnected or isolated from staff?
- Do I listen to learn from all team members, or do I selectively listen to those who say what I want to hear?
- Do I show care and concern for all people—students, staff, and community members?
- Do I readily acknowledge my mistakes and own the decisions I make?
- Do I get results?

PRACTICES TO STRENGTHEN FORWARD THINKING

As you have learned in this chapter, a critical, non-negotiable trait for effective, credible leadership is being a forward thinker. Workers around the globe, in a wide variety of jobs, of all ages and demographic backgrounds, listed *forward looking* as the trait they most admire in leaders, just behind *honesty*. People, in nonprofits especially, are looking for organizations that offer the workforce a clear direction, an inspiring vision, and meaningful work for the greater good. They want to be members of synergistic teams in which together they accomplish more than they ever could alone. Below are suggested strategies that may strengthen your ability as a forward-thinking visionary leader. At the end of this section, think about the Pause and Ponder questions that can help you decide how to proceed in becoming a forward thinker.

Build a learning culture in your school. As you have learned throughout this chapter, leaders cannot be forward thinking if they instead are sticking their heads in the sand. Rather, we have to send the periscope up, outside of our schools or districts, to look around, check out the landscape, and understand the forthcoming issues, challenges, and new information that may impact what we do and how we do it day in and day out. This means that leaders have to spend dedicated time, as scheduled items on their calendar, to learn, read, and speak with experts in the field. You need to be connected to networks outside of your district to be exposed to new and different ways of thinking about upcoming challenges.

As important, leaders must model professional learning within the school. Become a teacher among teachers, become a learner among learners, and encourage and support others in doing what you are doing to be "future ready." Make it clear that the number one job of everyone in the school is to learn as much as they can about being better every day for the learners who walk through the doors deserving the very best education you can offer.

Collaborate with staff to create an inspirational vision for the future. Start this work with the leadership team or a small group of interested staff members where new research is shared, interesting articles are discussed, and collective learning takes place. Follow these meetings with visioning meetings for the staff to share their hopes and dreams about the future of the school. Determine if there are patterns in these hopes and tie them to outcomes you desire for students.

Ask and discuss the answers to questions like *What kind of experience do we want our students and families to have at our school? What do we hope to accomplish by the time a student leaves us and goes on to their next step in life? What do we want to be known for around the community? What practices are right for our team as we strive for excellence?* Of course, you may have different questions you would ask, but the key is to collaborate with and value the input of staff members to create a vision for the future they find inspirational and worthwhile.

Take charge of your calendar and day's activities. If your calendar currently whips you around like a rag doll, stop and take charge of it. Yes, there are emergencies that arise during the day that must be attended to, sometimes by you. But stop and ask yourself, "Am I the only one capable of doing the things I am doing that keep me from more important leadership work?" Take the time to delegate tasks to members of your team who are capable and able to address them. Support their learning along the way and then let them work. Add daily routines to your calendar that include time for class visits, talking and visiting with students, and time for your own learning.

Lead with empathy. As you start to create a forward focus, be mindful to check in often with the people affected by it. Understand that not all people will jump on board at the same time or in the same way. Checking in on them conveys care and concern and, as you learned in Chapter 1, builds trust. Ask how they are feeling, what challenges they anticipate, and what apprehensions they have, and share your thoughts as well. This will help in forging strong bonds that will help get everyone through the tough times.

PAUSE AND PONDER

▶ Which of the suggested strategies above resonate most with you as a first step in becoming a forward thinker? Who on your staff are you thinking about sharing this work with?

THE WAY FORWARD

Now that you have come to the end of the book, we congratulate you on taking an interest in learning about leader credibility and taking the time to learn about ways you can strengthen your credibility with staff. There are many ideas in the previous pages. We encourage you to think about the aspects of credibility that are already strengths for you and then consider one or two next best steps on things you could improve. Remember, leadership is a complex and overwhelming endeavor. Have a plan, take deliberate steps, and enlist the help of trusted mentors, coaches, or staff members. We believe that you can do it and that you will realize significant benefits by engaging in this important development work.

APPENDIX

Leader Credibility Self-Assessment

TRUSTWORTHINESS					
ITEM #	SURVEY ITEM	3 ALWAYS	2 SOMETIMES	1 RARELY	0 NEVER
1.	I make intentional efforts to empathize with teachers and staff by asking how they are feeling and showing care and concern for them as individuals.				
2.	I ensure staff and other key team members know that I became a school leader to learn with and from them and that I enjoy my job most when they achieve.				
3.	I believe in the abilities and motivations of the staff and students.				

TRUSTWORTHINESS (Continued)					
ITEM #	SURVEY ITEM	3 ALWAYS	2 SOMETIMES	1 RARELY	0 NEVER
4.	I follow through on promises and statements I make to teachers, students, and parents.				
5.	I ensure that I provide accurate, credible information to all educational partners in the school community.				
6.	I create a risk-free climate where teachers and students can learn from mistakes and respect each other in learning.				
Mean for Trustworthiness *(Total divided by 6)*					

COMPETENCE					
ITEM #	SURVEY ITEM	3 ALWAYS	2 SOMETIMES	1 RARELY	0 NEVER
1.	I invest in my own self-development and strive to stay current on research for effective teaching and leading.				

ITEM #	SURVEY ITEM	3 ALWAYS	2 SOMETIMES	1 RARELY	0 NEVER
	COMPETENCE (Continued)				
2.	I demonstrate strong instructional leadership through well-organized, purposeful conversations with teachers about evidence-based teaching and learning practices.				
3.	I strive to provide clarity on instructional practices that work best and I provide feedback based on success criteria.				
4.	I prioritize time for daily classroom visits where I engage in conversations about teaching and learning with staff and students.				
5.	I drop in on PLC meetings to offer support and guidance to teams.				
6.	I seek and act on feedback from staff, students, and parents to improve the effectiveness of my leadership.				
Mean for Competence *(Total divided by 6)*					

DYNAMISM					
ITEM #	SURVEY ITEM	3 ALWAYS	2 SOMETIMES	1 RARELY	0 NEVER
1.	I am excited about the potential of my school to achieve great things and I effectively communicate this belief.				
2.	I enjoy engaging fully with my staff in professional learning, staff meetings, and other school events.				
3.	I am intentional about speaking with passion and excitement about the future possibilities for our school.				
4.	When appropriate, I use personal stories, relevant and interesting videos, pictures, slide presentations, articles, etc., to make messages come alive for all team members.				
5.	I seek and use feedback on how my staff perceives my levels of self-confidence and competence.				
Mean for Dynamism (Total divided by 5)					

IMMEDIACY					
ITEM #	SURVEY ITEM	3 ALWAYS	2 SOMETIMES	1 RARELY	0 NEVER
1.	My verbal and nonverbal communication signifies a genuine interest in others.				
2.	I am intentional about being accessible and visible to staff, students, and parents.				
3.	I enjoy being among staff and students and sitting with them at their tables and in their groups while they are working.				
4.	I strive for partnership relationships with school team members to enable joint effort and commitment to reaching school goals.				
Mean for Immediacy *(Total divided by 4)*					

FORWARD THINKING					
ITEM #	SURVEY ITEM	3 ALWAYS	2 SOMETIMES	1 RARELY	0 NEVER
1.	I routinely allot time for reading professional journals, listening to podcasts, attending webinars, going to conferences, and/or engaging in book studies to learn about trends and best practices in education.				
2.	I have communicated and collaborated with staff on a vision for the future that is both aspirational and inspirational for staff and students.				
3.	I engage the leadership team in conversations by asking questions like *What's new? What's next? What's better for our staff and students?*				
4.	I routinely collect and share evidence with staff on our progress toward our future state and collaborate on the next best steps.				

FORWARD THINKING (Continued)					
ITEM #	SURVEY ITEM	3 ALWAYS	2 SOMETIMES	1 RARELY	0 NEVER
5.	I intentionally demonstrate a sense of optimism and hope for a better future for our school, especially during tough times.				
6.	I show care and concern for the people I work with and try to demonstrate empathy in interactions.				
Mean for Forward Thinking *(Total divided by 6)*					

REFERENCES

Alt, M. (2019, September 6). *For credible leaders, perceiving is believing.* https://www.fox.temple.edu/posts/2019/09/for-credible-leaders-perceiving-is-believing

Balchandani, A., Beltrami, M., & Kim, D. (n.d.). Three qualities of the forward-thinking leader. *The Leadership Review.* https://www.leadershipreview.net/three-qualities-of-the-forward-thinking-leader

Blake, R. R., & Moulton, J. S. (1964). *The managerial grid.* Gulf Publishing.

Bottery, M. (2005). Trust: Its importance for educators. *Management in Education, 18,* 6–10.

Bredeson, P. (1987). Principally speaking: An analysis of the interpersonal communications of school principals. *Journal of Educational Administration, 25*(1), 55–71.

Bryk, A., & Schneider, B. (2002). *Trust in schools.* University of Chicago Press.

Bryk, A. S., & Schneider, B. (2004). Trust in schools: A core resource for school reform. *Educational Leadership, 60*(6), 40–45.

Burkhauser, S. (2017). How much do school principals matter when it comes to teacher working conditions? *Educational Evaluation & Policy Analysis, 39*(1), 126–145.

Cottrell, D., & Harvey, E. (2004). *Leadership courage: Leadership strategies for individual and organizational success.* Walk the Talk Company.

Dalonges, D. A., & Fried, J. L. (2016). Creating immediacy using verbal and nonverbal methods. *Journal of Dental Hygiene, 90*(4), 221–225.

Danielson, C. (2007). *Enhancing professional practice: A framework for teaching.* ASCD.

Davila, E., Holland, G., & Jones, J. (2012). Involuntary departure of Texas public school principals. *Research in Higher Education Journal, 16*(1), 1–10.

Ericsson, K. A., Krampe, R. T., & Tesch-Römer, C. (1993). The role of deliberate practice in the acquisition of expert performance. *Psychological Review, 100,* 363–406.

Fisher, D., & Frey, N. (2021). *Better learning through structured teaching: A framework for the gradual release of responsibility* (3rd ed.). ASCD.

Fisher, D., Frey, N., Almarode, J., Flories, K., & Nagel, D. (2019). *The PLC+ playbook: A hands-on guide to collectively improving student learning.* Corwin.

Fisher, D., Frey, N., Amador, O., & Assof, J. (2019). *The teacher clarity playbook: A hands-on guide to creating learning intentions and success criteria for organized, effective instruction.* Corwin.

Fisher, D., Frey, N., & Hattie, J. (2021). *The distance learning playbook: Teaching for engagement and impact in any setting.* Corwin.

Fisher, D., Frey, N., & Smith, D. (2020). *Teacher credibility and collective efficacy playbook.* Corwin.

Folkman, J. (2019, February 12). How self-confidence can help or hurt leaders. *Forbes.* https://www.forbes.com/sites/joefolkman/2019/02/12/how-self-confidence-can-help-or-hurt-leaders/?sh=454814855990

Folkman, J. (2021, July 15). Don't fake it 'til you make it: Match confidence to competence. *Forbes.* https://www.forbes.com/sites/joefolkman/2021/07/15/dont-fake-it-till-you-make-it-match--confidence-to-competence/?sh=28ecf9183a94

Foster, M. (2019, February 27). *Immediacy: Five ways to use it.* https://mafost.com/immediacy-5-ways-to-use-it

Fullan, M. (2019). *Nuance: Why some leaders succeed and others fail.* Corwin.

Glazer, J. (2018). Learning from those who no longer teach: Viewing teacher attrition through a resistance lens. *Teaching and Teacher Education, 74,* 62–71.

Goleman, D. (2006). *Social intelligence: The new Science of human relationships.* Random House.

Good, T. (1987). Two decades of research on teacher expectations. *Journal of Teacher Education, 38*(4), 32–47.

Gordon, T. (2003). *Teacher effectiveness training: The program proven to help teachers bring out the best in students of all ages.* Three Rivers Press.

Grant, A., Hann, T., Godwin, R., Shackelford, D., & Ames, T. (2020). A framework for graduated teacher autonomy: Linking teacher proficiency with autonomy. *Educational Forum, 84*(2), 100–113.

Grissom, J., Loeb, S., & Master, B. (2013). *Effective instructional time use for school leaders: Longitudinal evidence from observations of principals.* Vanderbilt University & Stanford University.

Gwaltney, K. D. (2012). *Teacher autonomy in the United States: Establishing a standard definition, validation of a nationally representative construct and an investigation of policy affected teacher groups* [Unpublished doctoral dissertation]. University of Missouri.

Hall, R. M., & Sandler, B. R. (1982). *The classroom climate: A chilly one for women?* https://files.eric.ed.gov/fulltext/ED215628.pdf

Hattie, J. (2015). High-impact leadership. *Educational Leadership, 72*(5), 36–40.

Hawkley, L. C., & Cacioppo, J. T. (2010). Loneliness matters: A theoretical and empirical review of consequences and mechanisms. *Annals*

of Behavioral Medicine, 40, 218–227. https://doi.org/10.1007/
s12160-010-9210-8

Hill, A. (2018). Leaders' credibility is fragile and easy to lose. *FT.com.*

Holmes, W., & Parker, M. A. (2018). The relationship between behavioural
integrity, competence, goodwill, and motivating language of a principal. *School Leadership and Management, 38*(4), 435–456.

Holmes, W. T., Parker, M., Olsen, J. J., & Khojasteh, J. (2021). The effect
of rural superintendent credibility on principal and district outcomes mediated by motivating language. *Journal of Educational
Administration, 59*(6), 776–793.

Jaca, N. I. (2021). The challenges of transitioning from teacher to department head in seven primary schools. *Perspectives in Education, 39*(3),
242–256.

Kingsley Westerman, C. Y., Reno, K. M., & Heuett, K. B. (2018). Delivering
feedback: Supervisors' source credibility and communication competence. *International Journal of Business Communication, 55*(4),
526–546. https://doi.org/10.1177/2329488415613338

Kouzes, J., & Posner, B. (2009). To lead, create a shared vision. *Harvard
Business Review.* https://hbr.org/2009/01/to-lead-create-a-shared-vision

Kouzes, J., & Posner, B. (2010). *The truth about leadership.* Jossey-Bass.

Kouzes, J., & Posner, B. (2012). *Credibility: How leaders gain and lose it:
Why people demand it.* Jossey Bass.

Kruse, K. (2016a, April 24). Why successful leaders don't have an open door
policy. *Forbes.* https://www.forbes.com/sites/kevinkruse/2016/04/24/
why-successful-leaders-dont-have-an-open-door-policy/?sh=30e8db-
5b31ef

Kruse, K. (2016b, May 2). Close your open door policy and do this
instead. *Forbes.* https://www.forbes.com/sites/kevinkruse/2016/05/02/
close-your-open-door-policy-and-do-this-instead/?sh=480cde47d2cd

Kuster, E. (2016). 9 traits optimists have in common. *Prevention.* https://
www.prevention.com/life/g20475084/9-traits-optimists-have-in-common

Lassiter, C. (2017). *Everyday courage for school leaders.* Corwin.

Mandal, F. B. (2014). Nonverbal communication in humans. *Journal of
Human Behavior in the Social Environment, 24*(4), 417–421.

Manna, P. (2015). *Developing excellent school principals to advance
teaching and learning: Considerations for state policy.* The Wallace
Foundation.

Marks, H. M., & Printy, S. M. (2003). Principal leadership and school performance: An integration of transformational and instructional leadership. *Educational Administration Quarterly, 39*(3), 370–397. https://
doi.org/10.1177/0013161X03253412

McCroskey, J. C. (2005). *An introduction to rhetorical communication*
(9th ed.). Prentice-Hall.

Mehrabian, A. (1971). *Silent messages.* Wadsworth.

Mehrabian, A. (1972). *Nonverbal communication*. Aldine-Atherton.

Myatt, M. (2015). *5 dead giveaways you're not a credible leader. Forbes Magazine*. https://www.forbes.com/sites/mikemyatt/2015/11/08/5-dead-giveaways-youre-not-a-credible-leader/?sh=33ce9b06ddd8

Nichols, M. P. (1995). *The lost art of listening: How learning to listen can improve relationships*. Guilford.

Northfield, S. (2014). Multi-dimensional trust: How beginning principals build trust with their staff during leader succession. *International Journal of Leadership in Education, 17*(4), 410–441.

Richmond, V. P., McCroskey, J. C., & Hickson, M. L. (2012). *Nonverbal behavior in interpersonal relations* (7th ed.). Allyn and Bacon/Pearson Education.

Robinson, V., Meyer, F., Le Fevre, D., & Sinnema, C. (2021). The quality of leaders' problem-solving conversations: Truth seeking or truth claiming? *Leadership and Policy in Schools, 20*(4), 650–671.

Robinson, V. M., Lloyd, C. A., & Rowe, K. J. (2008). The impact of leadership on student outcomes: An analysis of the differential effects of leadership types. *Educational Administration Quarterly, 44*(5), 635–674.

Ryan, R. M., & Deci, E. L. (2000). Self-determination theory and the facilitation of intrinsic motivation, social development, and well-being. *American Psychologist, 55*(1), 68–78.

Saiti, A. (2014). Conflicts in schools, conflict management styles and the role of the school leader: A study of Greek primary school educators. *Educational Management Administration & Leadership, 43*(4), 582–609.

Schmitz, T. (2016, October 28). *Empathy—Empathetic listening*. https://www.conovercompany.com/empathy-empathetic-listening

Schwabsky, N., Erdogan, U., & Tschannen-Moran, M. (2020). Predicting school innovation: The role of collective efficacy and academic press mediated by faculty trust. *Journal of Educational Administration, 58*(2), 246–262.

Seligman, M. (2006). *Learned optimism: How to change your mind and your life*. Vintage Books.

Shell, G. R. (2001). Teaching ideas: Bargaining styles and negotiation: The Thomas-Kilmannconflict mode instrument in negotiation training. *Negotiation Journal, 17*(2), 155–174.

Sinha, S. (2020, September 22). *Leadership credibility—Why it matters and how to develop it*. https://soaringeagles.co/resources/leadership-credibility-why-it-matters-how-to-develop-it

Slade, S., & Gallagher, A. (2021). Transformational vs. instructional leadership. Which is better? *Peter DeWitt's Finding Common Ground. Education Week*. https://www.edweek.org/leadership/opinion-transformational-vs-instructional-leadership-which-is-better/2021/10

Sullivan, J. (1988). Three roles of language in motivation theory. *Academy of Management Review, 13*(1), 104–115.

Sutherland, I. E., & Yoshida, R. K. (2015). Communication competence and trust in leaders. *Journal of School Leadership, 25*(6), 1039–1063.

Talley, L., & Temple, S. (2018). Silent hands: A leader's ability to create nonverbal immediacy. *Journal of Social, Behavioral, and Health Sciences, 12*(1), 128–139.

Torres, A. C. (2014). "Are we architects or construction workers?" Re-examining teacher autonomy and turnover in charter schools. *Education Policy Analysis Archives, 22*(124), 1–23.

Tucker, R. (2020). Are you a forward-thinker? Use these 4 questions to find out. *Forbes*. https://www.forbes.com/sites/robertbtucker/2020/10/08/are-you-a-forward-thinker--------use-these-4-questions-to-find-out/?sh=2e094687ea0a

Tschannen-Moran, M. (2004). *Trust matters: Leadership for successful schools*. Jossey-Bass.

Üstüner, M., & Kiş, A. (2014). The relationship between communication competence and organizational conflict: A study on heads of educational supervisors. *Eurasian Journal of Educational Research (EJER), 56*, 1–22.

Uzun, T., & Ayik, A. (2017). Relationship between communication competence and conflict management styles of school principals. *Eurasian Journal of Educational Research, 68*, 167–186.

Van De Vliert, E. (1998). Conflict and conflict management. In P. J. D. Drenth, H. Thierry, & C. J. de Wolff (Eds.), *Handbook of work and organizational psychology: Personnel psychology* (2nd ed., pp. 351–369). Psychology Press.

Wai, F. (n.d.). 18 practical ways to build trust in the workplace. *Jostle*. https://blog.jostle.me/blog/how-to-build-trust-in-the-workplace

Williams Jr., R., Raffo, D. M., & Clark, L. A. (2018). Charisma as an attribute of transformational leaders: What about credibility? *The Journal of Management Development, 37*(6), 512–524. https://doi.org/10.1108/JMD-03-2018-0088

Wilson, J. H., & Locker, Jr., L. (2007–2008). Immediacy scale represents four factors: Nonverbal and verbal components predict student outcomes. *Journal of Classroom Interaction, 42*(2), 4–10.

Won, L. S., & Bong, M. (2017). Social persuasions by teachers as a source of student self-efficacy: The moderating role of perceived teacher credibility. *Psychology in the Schools, 54*(5), 532–547. https://doi.org/10.1002/pits.22009

INDEX

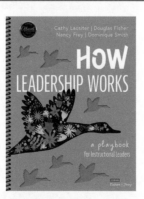
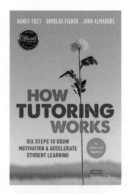

A SAGE Publishing Company

Helping educators make the greatest impact

CORWIN HAS ONE MISSION: to enhance education through intentional professional learning.

We build long-term relationships with our authors, educators, clients, and associations who partner with us to develop and continuously improve the best evidence-based practices that establish and support lifelong learning.